Cries From Within
revised version

He sent His word and healed them, and delivered them from their destructions.

-Psalm 107:20, New American Standard Bible
(italics added)

Nefateri Pecou Smalls

All scriptures are taken from various versions of the Holy Bible. The biblical references are indicated by translation and/or version.

CRIES FROM WITHIN revised version
Copyright © 2014 by Nefateri Pecou Smalls
Healing Hurts LLC
P.O. Box 231
Ridgeville, SC 29472
www.healingofhurts.org

All rights reserved. No part of this book may be reproduced, stored in a retrieval system, or transmitted in any form or by any other means – electronic, mechanical, photocopying, recording, or otherwise-without written permission of the author, Nefateri Pecou Smalls.

ISBN 13: 978-0-979486-1-73

Truth Book Publishers
www.truthbookpublishers.com
877-649-9092

Third Printing 2015
Revised Copy

Printed in the United States of America

DEDICATION

This book is dedicated to the memory of my mother, the late, Betty Ann Ridges Pecou, (1948-1980). I also dedicate this book to all of the broken, wounded, and abused. You WILL find healing in this book. Today is the beginning of your daybreak.

ACKNOWLEDGEMENTS

Like a complicated math equation, my life pays homage to so many lives before me, but the first and foremost honorable mention indeed goes to my risen Savior. He is indeed the pen that writes on the paper of my heart so that others will come to know who He is through me. I have travelled this road many times and oftentimes feeling very lonely. Yet in His appointed time, God saw fit to share a gift with me. I am so privileged to have my covenant partner, Oddie Smalls, who not only holds my hand, but my heart. You have wiped away tears, covered me in some of the most vulnerable seasons of my life, and you truly love me like Christ loves the church and gave Himself for it. Baby thanks for being so selfless and for helping me to laugh my way into purpose. I agree with Gods' will for our life and we WILL turn the world upside down together. (Acts 17:6)

To our children (Allen, Clifton, Alexis, Olivia, and Christy) who continue to help us to stay sane and focused in seasons when life would hope to weary us from moving forward. I bless God for my godmother Bishop Vera M. Davis who prayed and walked me through some of the most difficult times of my life. To Momma Connie & Dad Alexander Coe – always my parents...thank you for being consistent even when you didn't have to be. Perfect love indeed prevails.

To my biological Dad, Guillermo A. Pecou we both know that forgiveness and restoration goes beyond the dictionary. May we show the world how Christ loves us all. To my siblings who too have endured their own plight and challenges in growing up (Kwasi, Namibia, and Fahamu) may we all share love and hope by the message our lives preach to others. Lastly, but indeed not least at all Dr. Dexter and

Lady Leisa Easley – whose words of wisdom breathed life into me when I wanted to crumble in a corner and give up – God bless you. May God increase you for the love and hope you both have shared with me.

Chapters

One
The Breaking of Day — 8

Two
The First Sound of the Trumpet — 18

Three
The Lost Years — 25

Four
Two Steps Forward and Three Steps Back — 31

Five
A Stone Cold Romance — 36

Six
God, Why Me? — 40

Seven
Discouraged Soul — 49

Eight
Cries From Within — 54

Nine
The Beginning of the End — 61

Ten
Holy Visitation — 69

Eleven
Pulling Up The Rug — 75

Twelve
Soul Ties — 81

Thirteen
Breaking Free – 88

Fourteen
Escaped To Tell – 98

**SCRIPTURES QUOTED IN TEXT - 105

* Some of the names in this book have been changed to protect the rights and privacy of the actual persons involved. The contents of this book are solely shared to promote healing, restoration, and forgiveness while encouraging all to become a part of the Body of Jesus Christ.

One

The Breaking of Day

Yet in all these things we are more than conquerors through Him who loved us.
(Romans 8:37, NKJV)

Our earliest memories are often tucked away in the backs of our minds. When we think back, we find that many of these memories carry the fond feeling of family ties, childhood moments that you don't ever want to let go of, and hours of friendly gatherings that still make you laugh until your side hurts. And often underneath it all, there also lies a heaping mound of cobwebs that conceal those moments that are filled with guilt, shame, disgust, and defeat. Some of these guilt-ridden situations we have willingly walked into on our own, and then there are those situations that took place in which we had no control. We have parked ourselves at the door of don't ask and don't tell moments that we would be too disgusted to rehearse mentally less more to verbally repeat them to anyone else.

I learned a valuable lesson in life – in this lesson I have come to realize that even when we opt to say nothing, we have still said something. And sometimes our choice to be quiet makes us just as guilty as if we had done someone harm. So, with that in mind, I chose to speak. I'm sure you are probably thinking speak about what? Well…about the cobwebs. Those cobwebs that are so overladen with dust that you cringe at the sight of them. Or the ones that we hoped would never reveal some of the ugly truths about us, but in all honesty they have helped to make us into who we are. Everyone loves to close the door on these issues in hopes that they go away, but I'm different. And so you will find along these pages – so are you. But who says different has to be bad?

My earliest memories are scattered with visual snapshots of the streets in New York. I can hear the sounds of honking car horns, iron clashing down on packed snow that has stacked itself from inches to feet as neighbors work hard to shovel the snow from their driveways and entrance doors, and the distinct aroma of burning incense in our apartment. I don't know which was more intriguing to me….the thick fog that the burning incense left behind or the smell that it produced from room to room. When one incense burned down to nothing, there was always the lighting of a new one.

This repetitive incense burning made me think about the tenacity of my parents who both always appeared to be doing something. My parents were driven to be entrepreneurs. My mother was often nestled behind a sewing machine which is where we got most of our clothes. However, my father often ventured off to establish businesses of his own. They were trail-blazers in themselves, but even when you blaze your own trail, the bumps and bruises of life are not lessened.

January 10, 1980 is so embedded in my mind that I often wondered what parts of it I had made up and which parts of it held true. But as time would prove these cobwebs told no lies. My father who had just returned home from what I believed was a long road trip was barely interacting with us at all. He took these trips quite often, but my mother always seemed to hold it all down while he was away.

We ate our dinner without him that night because he was just too tired to come join us. The threats of a winter storm caused all of the train stations to hold their routes and subways were closed until further notice. Even though our home was heated, the draft of distance between my parents didn't take a meteorologist prediction. My brothers, sister, and I were lying in bed watching television. If I listened closely enough, I could hear my parents arguing. I suppose my father finally found the energy to wake from his rest, and from the sounds of their voices this was a rude awakening. Their voices seem to heighten the more they engaged in this disagreement. We were all hoping they would quieten down enough so that we can hear all of the lines for the show we were watching.

Even with all the laughter in our bedroom I could hear my mother crying. I was no longer interested in the next line of the show. By this point in time I was very concerned. It's funny how it doesn't matter how small you are, when someone or something is affecting your parents you feel as though you can take on the world. I was my mother's baby, so the curiosity of what was going on outweighed my desire to hang out with my siblings. I just had to see for myself what was going on. The closer I got to my parent's bedroom, the faster my heart would beat, and for some reason I was scared to walk up to the door. Once I arrived at the door I began to realize that I was no longer feeling afraid, but I was facing a fear that no child should ever have to see.

Being so young, I was trying my best to understand and accept what my eyes were beholding. My mother was lying flat on her back tussling with my father as he was straddled across her, repeatedly stabbing her in the chest.

I added to my mother's cry for help as I screamed out from fear. My father turned to look at me, and looked away as if he had not even seen me. The glare in his eyes told a story all on its own. I was jolted by my mother's voice as she yelled, "Kwasi, help me please," in between her yells from pain. Kwasi was my older brother and with no hesitation he came running in tears. "Ma, what's wrong," he responded sobbing. My father jumped and turned to look at my brother, and by this time we were all standing there crying. He yelled at us to get away from the door, and not to leave our room until he said so. My older brother and my mom were like the best of friends, so I could see the confusion in my brothers' face. He didn't know if he should run or stay and try to defend her. I guess considering the circumstances he didn't stand a chance. So, my brothers' and sister ran back towards their room screaming.

Unlike the others I just couldn't move. Something held me to that spot like glue. My mother then attempted to escape in an endless effort to get away from him. My father then stabbed her in the side and he asked my mom a question that baffled me for years, "Do you accept Jesus Christ as your personal Savior," he shouted!?

"Yes," my mom responded in a futile attempt to reserve her own life. Always before her answer was no. My father had become so bound by his circumstances, religion, and himself that he felt obligated to be her God. My mom realized that there was no way out unless she gave him the answer he wanted. At this point, I was crying even louder, and by this time my mother's cries were more like small gasps due to the fact that she had so many wounds to her chest. My father proceeded by lighting a fire to a substance that he poured around her bed. It was as if he was performing a ritual. The strangest thing however was that he didn't appear to be trying to burn her because the substance was too far away from her body.

My father then gathered us all up and we walked out of the apartment on feet. As we were leaving out of the building a few neighbors were peeping through cracks in the doors. They were trying to be nosy without being noticed. My father placed me up on his shoulders, and started walking. I remember the silence that night as we walked. We had no idea where we were going. My father did not attempt to bring anything with him other than his bible that he held clutched under his arm. On the way to wherever he was taking us we could hear the blaring sound of sirens. Words can't express how happy I felt in that moment. We could not help my mom, but looking over my father's shoulders and seeing the police and ambulance that drove past us, I knew they could. It burdened me to know that we had left my mom lying there like that. She needed help! I heard her say so myself. So, why were she and my daddy fighting in the first place?

I had a million thoughts racing through my head at the same time, but the one that resounded the loudest was why didn't my dad stay and try to help? Besides, he was the one that hurt her in the first place. He led us to the police station where he surrendered himself to authorities. And surprisingly enough, the bible he clutched under his arms was his alibi. I was so mad at my daddy for leaving her there, but the ambulance made it there in time to take her to a hospital, and I couldn't wait to go see her.

As we walked away leaving my mom
Lying there,
I felt like I was to blame.
Regardless of the fact that I couldn't
Really help -
Just the sound of her calling my name.
I wonder what she thought as she pleaded her case,
Which in exchange led to a piercing in my soul.
Did she stop to think that
The agony of defeat
Had opened its mouth to swallow her whole?
Or did she not care, but knew
In her heart that she was instilling in me
To stand strong and fight, no matter the cause,
But to believe in what I believe.
1 guess I'll just ask her when we return; when the police
Release us to go back home.
They've gotten us dressed and my aunt's on the way,
I heard him say so when he got
Off of the phone.
She explained to us that we would have
To go to her house
And stay there with her for awhile.
Until your mom gets back
on her feet,
she said.
So, of course this made me smile.

Like the download of lyrics to a cd, the images of that night were burned into the hard drive of my mind. This visual was more than enough to leave me stuck in the past. No matter how many obstacles or trials you have faced in life, you will always be left with the decision to run away from what you've dealt with, or to square your shoulders and push past what you have just encountered. When we go through life's struggles, it feels like we are at the end of our rope. I, too, have my share of mat-pinning moments. These are the moments when you are held down by the opponent (your obstacles), and instead of waiting on the referee (Christ) to declare that you have won, you would prefer to lay there in defeat and quit. I encourage you to just tap the wrestling mat of life and realize that you are more than a conqueror. What if I told you that the strength to win isn't in the fact that you are being held down? But as a man thinketh in his heart so is he. (Proverbs 23:7, KJV)

May I ask you just what you are thinking of yourself? Pause and think for a moment...the trial that you went through last month has prepared you for what you're going through right now. You would have never guessed that being called nobody or nothing could preset your identity today. Not because these words were spoken about you, but because you refused to believe what was said. Those same words have the power to extend the rope of tenacity to you. Will you take it?

This rope should not leave you hanging, but it helps you to break the bondage of fruitless words. When you reach for this rope of tenacity you are making a decision to live even while you're at deaths' door. Words of defeat are spoken in hopes to leave you crippled – making you unable to grow past them and on to the next phase in life. But today we render these fruitless words powerless.

It's hard to even imagine the agony that Christ endured as He faced crucifixion and hang upon the cross at Calvary, but He hung there for you and I. Our goal should be to strive to look like Jesus in spite of what our critics are saying. Christ's conduct at His crucifixion should motivate you to move from standing there bearing your heavy crosses to leaping in a sprint as we proudly suffer for the cause of Christ. Jesus was not swayed to show Himself powerful because of those who were calling Him powerless while they whipped Him. He did not feel the pressure to work a miracle and slay all of the men who persecuted Him as they mocked whether or not He was truly King. Nor was He compelled to explain to them who He really was, or even His assignment to them.

That's not to say that you should remain in an unhealthy environment. Unhealthy would be defined by you. You have to know when to stand still and when to move. For this cause, prayer is essential, so let us pray:

> Lord, I come on behalf of my brother or sister
> that is reading this book right now.
> First of all, we tell you thank you.
> Thank you for all that you've done,
> but most of all for who you are.
> Thank you for allowing this book
> to seed a prospect of hope in their lives.
> I thank you for today is the beginning of their daybreak.
> I thank you for who they are now, but most of all for who they will become.
> I lift this person up to you
> that you would give them peace in their world of chaos.
> I ask that you give them direction in every area of their life.
> I bind every stronghold that may hinder them
> from being the vessel that you have called them to be.
> I speak peace in the midst of the storm.
> Send forth your latter rain upon them right now as they

read.
Open their heart and mind to come subject to your will.
We love you, we bless you,
and will forever give your name praise.
In Jesus name we pray, Amen.

TWO

The First Sound of the Trumpet

*When my father and mother forsake me,
then the Lord will take care of me*
(Psalm 27:10, NKJV)

    While at the police station, my brothers, sister, and I sat there sobbing as the officers tried to comfort us. I remember sitting there shaking from being so under dressed. Our hurry to leave our home left us in undergarments, pajama pieces, and shoes. These scattered pieces of clothing didn't stand a chance against the New York wind. But we dare not complain.

Glancing over at our dad whose t-shirt and hands were soiled with blood caused us to fear our own fate at this point. After we were all calm we sat in the waiting area as the officers fed us ice cream and they rounded up toys for us to take with us. The officers' faces showed an array of emotions. There were some who were down right disgusted and others were understandably concerned.

    My mother's sister showed up at the police station as she was alerted by neighbors as to what had taken place. When my aunt got all of the information straight she took us to her home. By this time we were all exhausted and went straight to bed. When I awoke the next morning, I noticed that my oldest brother and sister were gone. I went into the kitchen and my cousin was over in the next room sweeping. I glanced over at him from the kitchen and he looked up at me and smiled.

"Hey girl, how you doing," he asked?

"Where are Kwasi and Mimi?" I asked.

"They went to visit their family down south." "Where's my mommy?"

"She's at work, she'll be home soon."

"I want some cereal."

"I'll fix you some; just sit down at the table. Your brother is in the back room watching TV, so when you finish eating you can go back there with him."

I sat quietly and ate my cereal. For some reason I just didn't think my mother was at work, but on the other hand my cousin had no reason to lie. In the back of my little three-year-old mind, I knew my mother had encountered some injuries from the night before. I wanted to ask questions, but I didn't quite know just what to ask. I didn't want to get in trouble for being in "grown folks' business."

Several days passed by and around that sixth day my brother, Fahamu, and I were being packed up to go and join my brother and sister in South Carolina. After we were all packed we all went to the train station. This had to be one of the longest rides of my life. We sat there with little notes tagged to our tattered brown matching wool coats. The notes explained where we were to go, and who would be there waiting for us when we got off of the train.

When we arrived in Florence, SC there was a relative there waiting to pick us up. As if we had not sat long enough, here we were riding once again. Hartsville was about thirty more minutes away, and this was our next destination. Compared to the time we spent on the train it seemed as if as soon as our ride in the car began it was time to get out.

Once we were at my great aunt's house, I received what I thought was the worst news of my life. My aunt talked to me for a little while and after she smoothed things over and broke the ice she said, your mother is dead!

I thought to myself..... dead...that's not possible...she was just at work...I just knew that I was going to crumble. The family tried to explain to us how no one knew what was best, but they did not think it was wise to have us at the funeral.

My best friend whom I trusted in to be there for me when I needed her had left me in this big, mean, and cruel world..... ALONE. Out of all the things that could have happened, this was the worst. How does a little girl become a woman with no mother? How am I supposed to go on? My heart began to beat so hard that I knew pretty soon it would come popping out of my chest. Reality began to strike my heart as I started to realize that I had lost my father too. Why did they lie to me? I did not want to go on, and as a matter of fact; I didn't think that I could.

I checked out mentally on life because I didn't see any real reason to go on. When someone experiences the loss of a parent, or both, it leaves behind what appears to be an unfixable void. Whether the loss is death, abandonment, or having your parents' physically but not emotionally there, you begin to wonder who you really are. You have nothing to tie you to who you are except pictures or significant others.

The goal then becomes to find someone or something to fill that void. And most of my life I acted as a leech on the back of its prey. My motive was to find a replacement for the parents I had loss. More too often the things we fill it with only act as a power drill. The more demand and strain you put on them to walk in shoes that are not theirs, they only dig a deeper void within you. Been there, and done that!!!!

Jeremiah 2:13 in the King James Version explains how we unawaredly we commit two evils:

1. We forsake the very God of heaven by not entrusting those dug out voided places to be filled with Him. He is the only living water that will not only fill us, but keep us from never thirsting again.

-OR

2. We take the voided areas of our life and fill them with what we think will be essential in the completion of us. Only causing those voided areas to act like a small hole of a tarred highway. Although that hole in the highway started out small, after it bears the weight of more cars, rain, and half-worked patching, it winds up becoming a pot hole. Deeper and more damaging than it was before. So what once was a small skip under the wheels of your tires as you rolled across it, it is now large enough and deep enough to cause your tire to explode upon impact. The very same thing that happened to this highway begins to happen within us.

We get so wrapped up in wanting to have someone physically be there until we forget about the omnipresence (everywhere at the same time) of God. We try filling those voids with other relationships, friendships, and false hopes. God designed our parents to conceive us, but they do not hold our destiny. I have heard so many people confess that they don't know how to parent because of the poor examples they had before them. I will admit that when your role models have been absent whether in body or mind it makes for a long road, but don't let excuses cripple you. Psalm 27:10 declares that when your mother and father forsake you, then the Lord will take you up. To forsake means to abandon or desert you. God wants you to know that your parents' loss was heaven's gain. God will be your father and mother and in turn teach you to be the same.

Try trusting in the hands of the One who can really hold you. Try standing on the shoulders of the One who will never let you down. He wants to be the one you go crying to when that man or woman breaks your heart, when you mess up at that recital, or when you didn't pass that math test. Sounds petty, right? He is all-powerful, and an awesome God He is, but having a relationship with the very one that holds your tomorrow does not take away from the fact that He wants to hear from you. This is a good place to lift your hands, open up your mouth, and begin to talk to Him.

I never knew that ones' heart
could endure so much pain,
and when I try to rid myself
life ends up just the same.
I've lost my inner glory, and
not sure of my outer pride.
I feel so all alone right now,
and it's inside that I cry.
I'm battling with fears that
I'm not quite so sure of what
they are.
Sometimes I feel like giving
up, but I realize that I've come
too far.
I feel so all alone right now,
I'm sure you can see why.
I'd rather hold in all my pain
than to sit around and cry.
I guess I'd better bow my head and
pray for the things I have instead of
those things that are gone,
but I wonder if that will help me
from feeling so alone.

Three

The Lost Years

> *Joseph called the firstborn Manasseh:*
> *For God has made me forget all my toil*
> *and all my father's house.*
> **(Genesis 41:51, NKJV)**

The next few years of my life literally felt like a living hell. I can't remember whether I was going or coming. I closed myself off from the world, and had no plan to come out. I went into my own little closet and I threw away the key. This hindered anyone from entering, but more importantly only I could permit myself to leave.

I stayed in this place for so long that I had lost touch with family, friends, and even myself. My memories of these years are not well at all, however, one thing stands true, the pain never went away.

During this time, I was seen by many therapists and psychiatrists. They tried to help me as best they could, but only harmed me more by not helping me to deal with the truth, but to override it all with lies. When I wasn't listening to the therapist I had to listen to family members tell me that I would end up crazy like my father.

My heart became so heavy from all the hurt and frustration that I held in. I didn't know how to release this pain that hurt me to such an extent. I felt vulnerable even at the thought of trying to face my pain. I blamed everyone and everything for what happened. I just wanted my mom to hold me and assure me that everything would be okay. No one sought to understand me so I was whipped when I cried too much. I was yelled at instead of consoled, and this left me even more broken than before.

There were some who tried to gain rapport with me in hopes that I would open up, and this made me close up even more. These were not the people that I wanted to talk to; I wanted my mother and father.

In order to survive there are valves in your body that have to open and close. I became like one of those valves. The very oxygen to my brain was being denied for fear the wrong thing would enter if I allowed that valve to be opened up.

I faced the ultimate hurt by losing my mom and dad, and for sure my heart could take no more. I would rather not have anyone if I couldn't have them. That's what I thought until I met Mrs. Denbark. She was our new elementary guidance school counselor. Whenever I would see her she was always smiling. There was something about her smile that made me feel so drawn to her. In her smile I saw a friend, I saw hope, and best of all I saw a mother. When she was around I felt no pressure to prove who I was or to be what I wasn't. She offered to love me as a mother, and my questions to her were:

> Pain and hurt is something my heart seems to endure.
> Is it okay to hurt mommy?
> Because right now I'm not sure.
> It seems as if someone's always picking
> to find my weak spot,
> depriving me of what I have,
> and making me what I'm not.
> Is it okay to hurt mommy?
> and sometimes shed a tear?
> Is it okay to be afraid?
> is it okay to fear?
> I'm scared to move on with my life

> sometimes it seems too late.
> I'm scared that tomorrows
> will turn out like yesterdays.
> I've found someone to listen,
> and I hope you're listening to me now,
> Is it okay to hurt mommy?
> is it okay to be down ?

I'm sure several of you can agree that there are portions of your lives that lie dormant inside. Times where there is no accountability for what happened in your life in those particular moments. This loss of short-term memory caused repression due to difficult or hurting times. Our mental being is manipulated when we encounter psychological trauma. It didn't make sense when I heard generations before me declare that God was a mind regulator, but now as I look back on it, there is no way that my mind could have been stabilized any other way. The absence of my parents took time to overcome, but in the process of my healing God allowed my heart to be touched by so many others who loved me without restraint or obligation.

I have heard people declare in prayer that God would take the pain out of the hurt. When you hear this phrase, pain and hurt seem to be contradictive of each other because how could you have one without the other? Have you ever cut your finger and at the time it may sting or burn? Then after you clean it up and wrap it, the pain eventually subsides. The next day you may push down on it and the impact of you pressing may be uncomfortable, but not painful. This is also how life can sometimes be. Although someone may address an issue that may have been sensitive to you in the past you are not brought to tears when you reflect on it anymore. A painful past may not have the same effect that it did before if it is dealt with properly.

When you present a wound to God, He then begins to take whatever steps are necessary in cleaning you up. John 15:3, NKJV declares you are already clean because of the word I have spoken to you. Did you hear that? You may not see it, but God has already declared that you are clean!

After a while the dirt of our past can cause us to feel that this is all we will ever know. I challenge you to present yourself to God in all the filth of your ways, the dirtiness of your thinking, and the garbage of your thoughts and see won't God clean you up. It's impossible to come into contact with the Savior and still stay the way that you are.

Many of us lose sight of God because there are those around us who have modeled a two-sided gospel. They are saved at church and they become what they want at home. We excuse our imperfections by saying God knows my heart so that we can still hold onto who we are. Every day is a new slate to strive towards perfection.

Does coming to Christ mean you will never hurt again, or that your failures and shortcomings will end? Absolutely not. But it does mean that there is hope and redemption where you once did not have any. You may just run into another bad relationship, or find yourself back in that same situation. For that cause, it may reopen a wound. If you find yourself back where you were, simply admit that you are just not there yet. One thing is for certain, you did not get into the situation you are in overnight, so you will need more than a quick fix to get out of it.

Acknowledging your brokenness and accepting your healing is only the beginning. You will still need to endure the process of walking in the manifestation of what you have already declared. So, stop being hard on yourself, and let the healing begin.

FOUR

Two Steps Forward and Three Steps Back

Brethren, I do not count myself to have apprehended; but one thing I do, forgetting those things which are behind and reaching forward to those things which are ahead, I press toward the goal for the prize of the upward call of God in Christ Jesus.
(Philippians 3:13,14, NKJV)

It was such a joy just to know that someone paid attention to "little 'ole me." Some days I had to question myself whether it was real for someone to be so concerned and love you so genuinely in so little of time. My great-aunt, whom I called grandmother, didn't allow me to do much, so we talked on the phone most of the time. Occasionally Mrs. Denbark would get permission to come and pick me up, and we would go to a play or liturgical performances.

I was always really creative, so I would write Mrs. Denbark little poems and make things for her desk because I didn't have money to buy her anything. Then the day came that I really didn't want to see - it was time for me to go on to Junior High, which meant I had to leave Mrs. Denbark. On the last day of school for the year my aunt came to pick my cousins and I up from school. As I sat in the car I looked over and saw Mrs. Denbark standing in the doorway of the school. When I thought I had caught her eye I leaned out of the window and shouted, "Hey, Mom, come here for a minute!" "Hold on one moment," she responded. She began to talk to some kids standing behind her, and started towards the car "Yes ma'am, you called," she asked? "I just wanted to see you before I left," I answered.

"Well, I have to go back in to finish cleaning my desk before I go."

"Don't leave me, please!"

"I'm not leaving you, you're leaving me," she said and turned to walk away.

Those words cut me so deep, and I couldn't understand why she talked to me like that. Didn't she know I would never leave her? I told her everything I possibly could about me and losing my parents was hard enough. Having experienced such a loss, does she not realize that I would never inflict the same pain on her that I had felt? I felt like I was back at square one. Another parent lost, and I couldn't do anything to stop it. Maybe it was something that I said? Now my heart began to question itself again...... where do I go from here?

So, I began to talk to God:
The tears I cry are many,
the love I feel is few.
Where do I go from here
I'm sure that I can count on you.
The pain I bear is heavy,
but it's no one's fault but mine.
Instead of looking forward,
I'm looking back in time.
The past brings back so much hurt,
and so many tears I've cried.
Through it all I was the victim
in this so-called life of mine.
Deep inside I hold a grudge,
and still I feel some fear
because I'm not very certain
of where to go from here.

It can often appear that the very time there seems to be

peace, you're then reminded of how much farther you still have to go. The mere thought of process causes hesitance in the heart of even the most prestigious person. When most people hear the word they come to a complete halt. Just think about that good cake or pie you had after dinner. I'm sure the baker did not just decide upon the cake, and it just mysteriously appeared. That cake went through a process. Even after all the ingredients are mixed there must be some heat applied to bring that cake to its perfected state. The cake has to stay in the heat for some time so that it is fully done. Then it is adorned with lovely icings and decorations. Just as that cake, God allows things in our lives that will bring us to be that which he has called us to be. Philippians 1:6, lets us to know that he that began a good work in you will carry it on to completion until the day of Jesus Christ. There will be some seasons of adding and some seasons where God will take some things away. There will be times of stirring and some of sweet bliss. It will even take some heat, but you proclaim to yourself every day that: I AM WHO GOD SAYS I AM!

This guidance counselor did not speak brutally to me, but I received it that way because I had not allowed myself to be healed fully. At this stage in my life I had no clue the extent of God's presence or love toward me. I heard everything through the ears of a 3-year old child who was scarred by a brutal domestic violence, along with verbal and emotional taunting. Many of us view the world through stained glasses. The glass is not stained intentionally, but life has been blurred by what we have encountered and everyone we meet reaps the aftermath of it. We expect every good thing to come to an end, we anticipate that our heart will get broken like it did before, and we hope that God thinks of us enough to give us enough money to pay our bills.

When God created you He had a plan in mind and as long as you allow Him; God will complete what He started. We are joint heirs with Christ. (Romans 8:17) The sooner we realize this, the sooner we will stop treating ourselves as if we don't belong.

As a joint-heir, the privileges and benefits allowed to us as kingdom citizens is all because we are connected to Christ. Your relationship with God is not based on merit. He's not waiting on you to live right for 365 days to overshadow you with His love. Romans 5:8 tells us that while we were yet sinners Christ died for us. You don't have to feel worthy in order for God to declare you to be worthy. He proved His confidence in you through His act of undying and selfless love. Everybody is not out to hurt you. However, our lives can be shaped by our experiences in a negative way if we are not subject to the freeing power of God.

You must change your mentality to believe that it does not matter that no one spoke into your life, because the power of life and death is in your tongue, make your own confessions. (Proverb 18:21) For that cause, you speak life to every dead situation that is essential in your completion. Invite God into your heart, and then invite Him into your situation.

Do not allow yourself to be governed by fear. Fear is defined as F-alse E-vidence that A-ppears to be R-eal. Go forth in the things that God has called you to.

FIVE

A Stone Cold Romance

> *I charge you, O daughters of Jerusalem,*
> *by the gazelles or by the does of the field,*
> *do not stir up nor awaken love until it pleases.*
> **(Song of Solomon 2:7, NKJV)**

I tried so hard to move on with my life, but I just couldn't let go of Mrs. Denbark. I was too afraid to lose another mother. One of my cousins that lived in the house with me went to the same school that Mrs. Denbark counseled, so I would write her letters and vice versa. When my grandmother found out, she didn't like the idea. For some reason she had this idea that my siblings and I would give someone else credit for what she had done. I eventually lost contact with Mrs. Denbark, but she definitely made an imprint on my heart. No matter what, I knew that God was not going to allow me to go through life without a mom. So, I just had to wait.

BACK AT HOME

My cousin Tiara and I did a lot of things together when we were younger, but eventually her mom stopped including me in on anything. I felt neglected because I couldn't understand why. My uncle didn't like the way things looked, so he and his family began to take up time with me. I would go and babysit his daughters while they worked around the house and ran errands. My life was finally falling into place. I gained a mom, dad, and even more siblings.

Even though I was babysitting, I always felt like I could be a child when I was around them. They made me feel loved. My presence wasn't an indication that I was a burden, another mouth to feed, or an object of someone else's abuse.

After my mother's death my family decided that having my siblings and I grow up in the same home was the best thing to do, so were raised by a family member. Even though we grew up in the same house we coped with not having our parents in our own way. Our caretaker was the type that loved to fuss a lot. She would keep us clothed and fed, but behind closed doors things were all torn apart from the nonstop verbal abuse that ate away at my heart. I would lay awake at night and hear the things she would say, and the names she would call me play over and over in my head.

During the summer of my eighth grade year, we relocated to a new residence. We began to attend a new church because we were on another side of town. I joined the choir and became a frequent member. After one particular concert, one of the members of the choir came over to talk to me. Mrs. Gertrude Dials was a very sweet and pretty lady, and I was even more excited when I found out that she was my Junior High School loves' mom.

Shortly afterwards, her son, Dominic Dials, and I began to talk on the phone, and we became very close friends. In Junior High it was an honor and a privilege to be paid some attention to by an older guy. I thought that Dominic was the best thing that had ever happened in my life up until this point.

I loved this guy for what he represented because the trail of hurt left by my past was no road map to a relationship. Love isn't love until it's given away is the beginning of a phrase, yet it is evident that this phrase should go both ways. I've experienced times when I did everything but lie under the front wheel of a man's car because I didn't know how to love nor did I know how to open up so someone could truly love me. However, this junior high fling was only the beginning of my relationship drama.

I thought it was okay to be messed up and messed over by a man. My goal was to stand there and do my part regardless of how the man treated me. I declare just as Solomon did in the preceding scripture at the opening of this chapter that there is no true love without self-restraint and ethical responsibility. The two animals mentioned in Song of Solomon 2:7 are significant because they are not tamed and they belong in the wild. They follow their own instincts. Many of us follow our own instincts when it comes to our hearts. We have no accountability, and we are convinced that others' experience is not enough to suffice for our own. So we head out to experience life with no self-restraint or ethical responsibility. I venture to tell you that maturity is not deemed by our legal age of 21, but our ability to make mature decisions when we find ourselves in situations that warrant us to do the opposite.

Love between a man and a woman is not devised to hurt you; it is mutual. Love is strong, but never forceful. Love joins a man and a woman in common union that they may come to know God in the fullness.

The reason why love to many of us produces drama and stress is because we have derived at our own definitions of what love is. And although these definitions are not fully inaccurate, they do have their flaws. This inaccuracy could be our view of love towards ourselves and/or others. Due to these flaws we find ourselves back in the arms of the abusive man, the drug addict, or the imbalanced man. God places people in your life to bless you, but God moves people out of your life to protect you, so count it all joy.

SIX

God, Why Me?

But seek first the kingdom of God and His righteousness,
and all these things shall be added to you.
Therefore do not worry about tomorrow,
for tomorrow will worry about its own things.
Sufficient for the day is its own trouble.
(Matthew 6:33, 34, NKJV)

It was now time for me to go to Senior High, and I was so ready. My newfound church family and crush had me feeling like I could conquer the world. For the first time in my life I felt like life was working in my favor. I could silence the daily verbal attacks from my grandmother with my euphoric fixes of church services and moments with my boyfriend. Unfortunately, my ninth grade year didn't start out like I thought it would. I had gone to my aunt and uncle's house and watched their kids like I always did. When it was time for me to leave, my cousins were asking to ride with us. My aunt was preparing them for bed, so my uncle told them that they would not be able to go this time. I stayed later than usual this time and I could not wait to get home and get into my bed.

On the ride home my uncle and I began to hold a conversation about life, and how things were actually going for me. The conversation was really getting strange, especially when it started to sound something like this:

"How are things with you and your boyfriend," he asked?
"We're fine," I responded.

"Do you ever kiss? You can tell me, I won't tell your grandma," he continued.

Being that it wasn't any of his business, I told him no.

"Do you know how to drive?" He went on to ask.
"No" I replied abruptly.

He must have noticed my hostility with him trying to ramble in my personal life about things I had no desire to discuss with him, so he decided to talk about driving. He told me he would let me drive one day on a country road where there's not much traffic. I responded with a simple shrug of my shoulders.

My uncle then pulled over on the side of a road and asked me to come and sit on his lap to get a feel of the steering wheel, as he controlled the brakes and accelerator. I started out hesitantly because I was a little nervous. My uncle reassured me that he would help me if I got too nervous, but before I could really concentrate that I would have to relax more. As I relaxed a little I felt his hand brush across my side. For some reason this touch didn't seem to be innocent, but I didn't pay it any attention because I was on his lap, and in my mind I thought that he had mistakenly touched me.

"You're really doing good," he said.

"Are you sure you haven't driven before?" he asked enthusiastically.

"No, I'm positive. Besides, whose car would I drive?" I responded laughing.

"Just keep your eyes on the road because you know if you drive off of the road both of us will get killed. So, no matter what happens; keep your eyes on the road."

His last statement puzzled me, but it was nothing to dwell on. I guess he was preparing me to not only be cautious, but to look out for the other drivers as well. Then he unexpectedly put his hand between my legs and asked, "Has anyone ever touched you down here?"

I automatically froze up and said nothing at all. I could not believe he did that. My long pause prompted him to ask me again and I just shook my head no. I began to pray in my heart because I didn't know exactly what he was going to do next. I reached over towards the car door because I thought that this was my only way out. So, my first instinct was to jump out of the car.

My uncle then grabbed my hand and said very persuasively, "You don't want me to let you do that now do you? You're not ready to die, so don't do that." He removed my hand from the door and placed it back on the steering wheel. Placing his hands back between my legs he asked,

"How does this feel?"

I just knew my life was over. I figured that if I kept quiet he would realize that I was uncomfortable with what he was doing.

"I know you like it; you don't have to tell me. It feels good to me, so I know it must feel good to you. Ooooh, you're so warm down here," he continued.

I then begin to move my legs around in hopes that he would stop. He took his hand and grabbed hold to my genitals tightly, and ordered me to be still. I began to cry on the inside as he ripped my panties in the seat and inserted two of his fingers into me forcefully as he said, "You're making me hot. I have never felt anyone so warm. You feel good on the inside. Did anyone ever tell you that? Did anyone else get a chance to experience this besides me?"

I began squirming my legs from side to side and this caused the car to swerve around in the road. He yelled at me in a loud voice and slammed on the brakes. By this time I was dying on the inside.

"I told you to keep the car on the road, now pull over," he shouted!

"I'm ready to go home," I responded sobbing.

"I said pull the car over on the side of the road!" he continued to scream.

I pulled the car off to the side of the road in front of an abandoned building. After he threatened to hurt me, he began taking off my clothes. After he had me completely undressed, he began fondling me. I would try to move, but he pinned me down with his arm. He then shoved his fingers into my vagina as he shouted obscene things to me. I began to holler, and I blanked out.

When I came to, my uncle was hovered over me putting my clothes back on. Once he saw that my eyes were opened and I seemed to be okay, he stroked his hand across my sweaty face and had the nerve to ask me if I wanted to drive the rest of the way home.

After I convinced him that I did not want to drive, he started towards my house. The rest of the ride home was quiet, outside of the time my uncle spent trying to persuade me not to say anything about what he had done. We finally reached my house and I hurriedly got out of the car as he met me on my side of the car, and shoved some money in my hand.

I walked up to the door slowly because in my mind I was baffled, in my heart I felt betrayed, and in my soul ... discouraged.

> As he forced himself within me
> He broke through my very soul,
> And as I cried out for forgiveness
> I still did not feel whole.
> How could I be so stupid?
> I knew what he wanted to do.
> But I allowed my mind to take over my soul,
> And I let the devil through.
> His kisses were just like fire
> That stung upon my neck.
> My soul just shattered within me,
> And now my life is a wreck.
> After he was done and over
> I saw a dark figure pass me by,
> And it looked back and shook its head,
> And simply questioned,
> Why?
> I then tried to befriend it, and I sat it upon my knee,
> And before long I began to realize
> That this discouraged soul was me.

This chapter to some may be too graphic. Some may even say it does not take telling it all to get to the point. I was intentionally trying not to skate around the issue though. When there is a soul at stake my intention is to be as transparent as possible that a soul may be won to Christ. My aim is not to depress you or to cause you to feel sorry for me. My point is to show that man, woman, boy, or girl that the same God that healed me, will heal them.

I gave this particular testimony to release to someone that just because a person may look flawless on the outside there were some things that had to be done to bring them to this point. A lot of times when someone goes to a church they see well-dressed people with uplifted hands, praises going forth, and people falling out under the anointing. The first impression of the individual who has their own struggle going on is: I'm not good enough for this place.

I didn't just get saved yesterday, and it took years for me to get to the point where I would openly share my testimony with anyone. Yet, while I was in the process of being made whole I would make an exchange in God's presence by offering Him me. When I gave my life to Christ my praise became indicative of my gratitude towards Him. In this praise I was celebrating God according to the promise that He would heal the hurt of my heart.

Even though I had found an outlet to my pain, it took time to complete a process. There were times when my lights were turned off, yes, my bills went unpaid, yes, I've had cars that were repossessed, yes, I didn't have a place to stay, yes, I've looked on the floor of my car to find $0.25 just to buy a bag of chips, so that I would have something to eat. I promise you that you are not alone. I've even had days where I declared a day of fasting because I knew I had no money to eat. I allow myself to be made transparent so you will know that you are not alone.
There have been days when I questioned my life. I felt almost like Job. Job is a biblical character whose life portrays

one of a man that is committed to God and in the matter of a day he lost his cattle, his house and all its belongings as well as his children. I, too, had lost everything and everyone that ever mattered in my life except for my sanity. And after this last incident I had lost another father too.

I'm often reminded of how Job's sorrows began. God released Satan to afflict him. God only questioned Satan to compel him to confess. Satan cannot do a thing to you baby, without permission from YOUR Savior, YOUR Deliverer, YOUR God.

The trials that we have faced and will face are not to see if we will fail, but our faith should be strengthened as we go through. There are even some situations that God has to teach a lesson to. The lesson that He's teaching in those situations seemingly designed to destroy you, is that no matter what happens that He has your back.

So, when you begin to question God, why? What is the purpose for this trial? Remember that the devil may have meant it for bad, but God meant it for your good. (Genesis 50:20) Everything that happens in your life may not have lined up to God's will, but I promise you........you are right on schedule!

> I thought about it and dreamed it,
> but knew it couldn't be.
> Until it hit me in my face
> That my dream was a reality.
> I tried to brace myself
> and hold it all in,
> But how could someone so dear to me
> commit such a sin?
> A family member, my uncle,

A dear and close friend,
Took advantage of what I thought
was love for him.
I'm standing here helpless
not knowing what all this is about.
Should I keep quiet and stand strong,
Or let this pain out?
I understand it'll hurt
no matter which way I go,
But what I sowed to reap this,
Lord, I don't know.
I was scared I couldn't stop him.
What could I say?
I wish I could've stopped him,
but there was no way.
I twisted and jerked,
But that did no good.
I should've stopped him.
I would've if I could.
It's too late now
to make an excuse.
There seems to be
nowhere to go
For those sexually abused.
I try different things
to get rid of the pain,
it goes away for a while
Then it's back to hurt me again.
I'm still hurting from back then can't you see?
I shouldn't question the Lord,
But God, Why Me?

SEVEN

Discouraged Soul

> *Why are you cast down, O my soul? And why are you disquieted within me?*
> *Hope in God,*
> *for I shall yet praise Him*
> *for the help of his countenance.*
> **(Psalm 42:5, NKJV)**

When I went into the house that night I gathered up my nightclothes and headed towards the restroom. I stripped off all of the clothes I had on, and what was left of my panties, and buried them at the bottom of the trashcan, balled up on the floor and whimpered to myself.

I began to question myself: "Why did this happen? I can't believe I did this to myself. You're so stupid, you're so stupid!! Why didn't you try to fight him? Why didn't you do something, I questioned myself?"

Some of the things my uncle said to me pierced my heart like a knife. I began to mouth those same obscene things to myself. I began hitting myself and pulling my hair. I didn't want anyone to hear me, but at the same time I wanted to be heard. I hurriedly got myself together, and went to bed. I pulled the covers over my head and cried myself to sleep.

By the next day, I had convinced myself that it was all completely a dream. I carried on as I would any other day. All of the family was coming over for a Labor Day cookout that we had planned. I woke up, took a long shower, and after getting dressed I began cleaning up the kitchen. As I was washing dishes, my uncle came in and joked around with everyone as usual. When the kitchen was clear my uncle came over to me and asked, "Did you tell anyone about last night?"

My eyes popped open, my heart dropped, and I had a lump in my throat so big it was unbearable. I simply looked at him and turned away. He grabbed my hand and placed a stash of money in it. It took everything in me to keep it together. I walked into the bathroom, lifted the toilet seat, and flushed the money down. I didn't want anything that tied me to him.

So many thoughts were running through my mind. For sure no one would believe me. It was all my fault. I should have never wanted to drive in the first place. How would I explain ever sitting that close to him anyway? I had convinced myself that it was only a dream, but I'm afraid THIS was a dream come true.

"Statistics show that 1 in 4 girls and 1 in 6 boys are sexually abused by their 18th birthday. Over 90-95% of all sexual molestation is committed by someone the child knows or trusts."
www.thechildcenter.com/resources/statistics

Many of us feel like we cannot move on without having the perpetrators apology. If I can be honest with you that day may never come. So let me apologize on their behalf: I am sincerely sorry that they did not know the jewel that was in their midst. I am sorry that they took an unjust liberty to gratify their own sinful nature. I apologize for the many nights you've cried, the broken relationships you have suffered, and the continuous bouts of suicide you have encountered at the negligence of someone else. The act is over now and its time to move on to the next step. Forgiveness. Forgiveness is really for you and not for them. Let me assure you that there is life beyond this. You were victimized, but you are not a victim. I know because you are holding onto this book.

At some point in life you begin to take your eyes off of the situation and try to focus on the silver lining. You begin to think to yourself that there is no way that there is a God that is just allowing you to go through like this. And if He is there, then where exactly is He? There are times when it seems as if He is just sitting there watching.

What He was actually doing was preparing you for such a time as this. He preserved my life and as a result I can boldly speak into your life and help you to realize that what happened to you doesn't define who you are. God knew that at the time that I watched my mother die, when I was let down, and when I was sexually abused that I would have to minister to you. This chapter is not saying to you that God did these things to develop my ministry, but because I've gone through it, He will use it for His glory.

Romans 8:28 – and we know that all things work together for good to those who love the Lord, to them who are called according to his purpose.

You've tried everyone and everything to solve your problems, but they have all failed you. For a moment though, there may have been that one someone or something that positively crossed your path like my uncle. On the inside I just knew I'd found the answer. His role as a father figure had filled a void that I longed for, and with the same intent to gain my trust – he manipulated me.

There were many who were not at all pleased at my honesty in this situation, and as disappointed as they were, it did not pale in comparison to the disappointment I felt. Yet, I often think to myself sometimes where I would actually be if I had the people in my life that I longed for, and those that

I thought I needed at the time I cried out for them most. I would probably be so wrapped up in them that I would not even know God for myself. Life has taught me to build my hopes on nothing less than Jesus blood and righteousness. I dare not trust the sweetest frame, but wholly lean on Jesus name. On Christ the solid rock YOU stand because all other ground is sinking sand!

   www.faithalone.org/journal/1998i/Ward

EIGHT

Cries From Within

*And for me, that utterance may be given to me, that I may
open my mouth boldly to make known
the mystery of the gospel,
for which I am an ambassador in chains;
that I may speak loudly, as I ought to speak.*
(Ephesians 6:19, 20, NKJV)

Later on that evening our Labor Day cookout began. Mrs. Dials was there, and I went through a long process of thinking. Should I tell her....no, she won't believe me....maybe I'm still dreaming. What will she think of me? Will she say that it was my fault? I went on like this for hours, but I finally muscled up enough strength to tell her to call me when she got home.

That night the phone rang. Luckily everyone was outside on the porch, so I felt assured when I answered the phone that I could talk like I needed to. And just as I was hoping it was Mrs. Dial's voice on the other line.

"You asked me to call you, is everything alright?" she asked. "No, there's something I think that I should let someone know, but I'm afraid," I responded in fear.

"Well, you know that you can always count on me. Whatever or whenever you call, you know I'm always here, so, come on, tell me what's going on," she continued.

Before I knew it, I was all in tears just telling her what had happened between my uncle and I. I began to tell her how I just wanted to die because all men were no good and nothing to me. At the same time I was trying to be quiet so that no one in my house could hear me.

"Nefateri, Nefateri," she screamed – just loud enough to get my attention. "Calm down! Oh, baby, I wish I could just come and hold you right now, but you and I both know how your grandmother really feels about me.

"Have you told anyone else besides me," she asked?

"No, ma'am, but you can tell them because I won't be here to do it," I stated.

There was a brief silence, then Mrs. Dials said calmly, "Let me tell you one thing -I love you!"

"Do you hear me? Please don't do this to yourself."

"You are a very sweet and pretty young lady; tell that devil to get behind you. You are a child of God!"

In the midst of her talking I felt comforted, but it wasn't enough because the hurt, confusion, betrayal, and pain were all still there. My mind began to wander away from our conversation to the noise I heard in the background. My family was discussing something about my sister who was away at college. I heard someone mentioning using the phone, and I almost broke my neck to say goodbye and to get the phone back onto the hook before I got caught. The last thing I needed was for them to question me about who I was on the phone with and what we were talking about.

After I hang up the phone I ran into the bathroom and began to beat on myself again. I felt like there was no one to blame but me. I looked over in the corner and saw a handle to some appliance and I remember thinking to myself, you may as well go on and do to yourself the very same thing that your uncle did to you with that appliance. It doesn't matter whether or not you cause damage to your pelvic area. Besides, who wants to marry a no good, dirty, used up slut? Who wants to date a girl who has been played over by her uncle?

> There's a battle within my soul
> That I wish I could get rid of.
> I wish that I could conquer it
> With someone's motherly love.
> I promise you it's not as easy
> As it seems to be.
> If only someone would open up
> Their heart and listen to me.
> Sometimes I wonder how far in life
> I'll ever get to go.
> But, I'll have to learn to realize
> That God is the only one who knows.
> I'll keep my hands in his hands
> And continue to fast and pray.
> Hold on to my hopes and dreams
> To make sure they don't fade away.
> I'm going to keep on striving to get
> As far as I can get,
> For I know the Lord won't fail me
> Because He hasn't failed me yet.

The next few days of my life I was in denial. I would do any and everything to occupy my time. At home I would go to the restroom and just sit there and cry as long as there were tears to cry, and when those tears dried up I spent the rest of the time praying for my life to end. My boyfriend noticed that there was a change in me as well because I wouldn't allow him to touch me anymore, so he broke up with me.

And even though it was another man walking out of my life, by this point I didn't even care. He had successfully done what every other reputable man in my life had done before me – leave.

My family acted as though I wasn't even there. Did they not notice that I was always in the restroom? Could they not see that even with all of my clothes on I felt so vulnerable? I hardly went to class because I was always somewhere crying. My friends did their best to console me, but they didn't know what was going on, and I could not bear to tell them. While in my English class one day at school I was writing a letter to tell someone what had happened. I didn't know who I would give it to, but I had to tell someone. There was no way I could go on hurting the way I was.

In the midst of my writing, my teacher must have noticed I wasn't paying attention, and during her lecture she walked up behind me. Without warning she quickly took my notebook from under my hand, and began to read it. Where was that hole in the floor when I needed it because this was the perfect time to escape it all? She kept my notebook until after the bell rang for the next class, but as everyone one else was leaving she asked me to stay behind for a moment. She walked me into the teacher's lounge and grabbed me by the hand. She looked me in the face and asked,

"Is this something you're just writing, or did this actually happen?"

Her question was preceded by a long silence as I stood there staring down at the floor. She placed her hand under my chin and lifted my head.

"Look at me," she said.

Tears began to stream down my face, and I could tell that she was at a lost for words.

"Nefateri, its okay. I'm here," she continued.

She placed her arm around my waist and pulled me close to her as she comforted me.

"From your reaction I can tell that this is not a story. I really hate to do this, but I am required by law to report this or I can lose my job. I have a free period later on today, can you stop by?" she asked.

I really just wanted to lie on the floor, kick, and scream. I wanted help, but this wasn't the way I wanted to get it. My grandma is going to kill me for sure, or better yet, I am going to kill myself. I didn't know where to begin, so I just shook my head yes. I was so scared! I literally got weak. She told me that she would have to keep my notebook as proof, and to come back later on in the day. I walked out of the lounge and proceeded hesitantly down the hallway. What in the world could go wrong next?

For years I was afraid to speak on the things that God had delivered me from. So, I held it all inside. I begin to feel like a prisoner to my very own issues, and the weight of it all was draining the life out of me. The weight was draining me because instead of trying to hold it in, I could be using my testimony to help strengthen someone else who may have been going through. What good is a testimony if you don't share it? My ministry was becoming as stagnant water on the inside of me. I was then reminded of St. John 7:38; He that believeth on me as the scripture hath said, out of his belly shall flow rivers of living water. (KJV)

My mission then became how to go about releasing the word that God had placed in my belly. Don't allow fear to keep you from sharing your testimony. You have nothing to fear, but fear itself. I'm reminded of the time the Lord led me to pray for a family member that had been stricken with cancer. I believed God for his healing, but he was still in a wheelchair. This troubled me a little, but God spoke to me and said the wheelchair is not his crutch, but his testimony. Just because you lean on that very thing that God used in delivering you that does not mean you cannot function nor does it mean that you are not free. The wheelchair is to show to others that he's been through something, and the fact that he is still alive proves his existence and Gods ability to sustain him in an otherwise hopeless situation. Don't let the very thing that God used in delivering you become a hindrance to your ministry. When you do this, what you will then find yourself doing is making an excuse for not going forth. It takes effort and pressing to birth your ministry, and pressing is pushing. So PUSH, until something happens. Be reminded that because you went through this and came out you should feel compelled to reach back and grab someone else. Someone needs to hear your testimony so that they too can gain strength and be made whole.

NINE

The Beginning of the End

> *But recall the former days in which,*
> *after you were illuminated, you endured a great struggle*
> *with sufferings:*
> *partly while you were made a spectacle*
> *both by reproaches and tribulations, and partly while you*
> *became companions*
> *of those who were so treated;*
> *for you had compassion on me in my chains,*
> *and joyfully accepted the plundering of your goods,*
> *knowing that you have a better and an enduring*
> *possession for yourselves in heaven. Therefore do not cast*
> *away your confidence,*
> *which has great reward.*
> **(Hebrews 10:32-35, NKJV)**

A few weeks later, I came home from school and two of my cousins, my brother, and grandmother were sitting on the porch. My grandmother called for me to come there. I knew something was going on from the expression that everyone had on their faces. For the past few weeks I had been petrified of coming home knowing that one day she would get the call concerning the letter I wrote.

"What's wrong?" My grandmother asked.

I looked at her puzzled and in return asked, "What do you mean?"

My whole body froze up, and I felt as though I had broken into a cold sweat. I knew exactly what she was talking about. I stood there and I could see my grandmother's lips moving, but I couldn't hear a word she was saying. To be honest, I didn't want to.

At that point the only thing I desired was for the earth to open up and swallow me whole. My ears had become numb, my heart raced, my hands felt sweaty, and my knees had gotten weak. I backed up towards the wall and started crying. It felt as though I was about to have a nervous breakdown.

"I told Fahamu when it happened, but he laughed," I shouted.

I felt like if I just said it loud and fast then it wouldn't be as bad. Only to realize that it didn't make any sense.

"Told Fahamu what," my grandma asked.

"About what Uncle Craig did," I managed to say sobbing. Apparently when I said this, my brother felt bad because he looked over at me, stretched his eyes, and said, I did think that you were playing.

A few days after my teacher took my notebook I couldn't hold it anymore, so I had to confide in someone. So, I told my brother Fahamu, but he apparently felt like I had made this up. My grandmother instructed everyone to go into the house except for me.

That left she and I on the porch....ALONE. I told her what had happened, and she replied, I'll talk to your uncle about this, but until then you sweep this under the rug. I don't want to hear anything else about it,

I had dared not say no, so I shook my head yes, and went inside. I tossed and turned all night long and on the inside I felt so numb. It didn't matter that I had on clothes and covers over me. The fact that I had to expose my issue left me feeling just that…exposed. Before I knew it, morning had come, and it was time for me to get ready for school. Oh, how I longed for morning to come so that I could remove myself from the situation.

While I was at school I tried my best to remain unfocused on what was happening at home, and I was in no hurry to leave that day. But of course the moment arrived that I dreaded to face; the end-of-the-day bell rang. When I arrived home, my heart began to race again because as I was approaching the house I saw my uncle's vehicle parked in the yard. I walked up the porch steps, spoke to everyone, and rushed into the house. I fumbled around trying to find something to preoccupy my mind. Moments later my grandma came in and asked me to come into her bedroom. Once I got there, she began to tell me that my uncle had denied everything, and that she didn't want to hear anything else about it. Her look of authority put a fear in my heart that left me speechless.

Tears welled up in my eyes and I felt so betrayed. The thing that bothered me most is that she believed him. She walked off and left me standing there and this only made me feel left at the scene of the incident again. I felt vulnerable, unprotected, and scared. Is this how it ends? My grandmother had drawn her conclusion to the matter and I had no say so in it. Truth be told, that was it. There was no more discussion to be had. He won!

Words could not contain the pain, misery, and hurt that I experienced from that moment leading on to the next few years. I felt as though God had put me on this earth for some type of punishment. Not only could I not control the things that were taking place in my life, but I also could not control those persons who crossed my path that caused these things to happen. But in spite of the abuse, the lies, the hurt, and the pain, I still managed to survive. I have taken my downfalls, stacked each one upon the other, and have climbed until I found myself where I am today. So, in spite of what happens in your life, let my life be an example that if you can take it, you can make it because everything happens for a reason...so they say.

Everything happens for a reason ...they say
it started when I was born within the month of May,
But everything happens for a reason so they say.
Then my father killed my mother one January day,
But everything happens for a reason so they say.
As things seemed to get better, unfortunately, I was raped,
But everything happens for a reason so they say.
I then became neglected by all that came my way,
But everything happens for a reason so they say.
My life came together after which I became saved,
And I struggled for years to overcome my fears from yesterday.
My mind stayed in confusion from all the things I faced,
but everything happens for a reason...they say.
As I reflect back on the things that God has brought me out of, I'm grateful...grateful that I gave my life to Christ. There are some that may have turned to alcohol, suicide, or drugs. I have a lot of people tell me that they feel silly talking to me about issues due to the things that I've faced. My retaliation for that is to whom much is given, much is required. If it were up to me, I would have picked the easier trials. My level of ministry is for those who were wounded, let down, and abused.
For that cause, the things that I have faced, better

equipped me spiritually. It doesn't matter how great or small the trial may appear to the next person.
There is no one sitting back weighing the weight of the trials in your life. God has equipped each one of us individually, yet uniquely.

As I was writing I asked God to help me to only say what He would have me to. The things in which God has allowed me to expound on is not to indicate to you that my whole life was awful. I've had just as many good days as bad.

I only use my life's testimony to declare to you that God is able. Not only is He able, but He's willing. Willing to deliver you, set you free, heal you, or whatever the need may be. I told God that my heart's desire is to have the #1 selling book on the market, but if lives aren't changed, it's not worth it. I'd rather sell five books, and make a difference in the lives of those five people. My prayer is that a soul is reached, and not only reached but delivered.

So, it's not by chance that you're reading this book. God knew that on this day you would be reading this. It was part of your destiny that your heart would be tilled as a farmer tills the soil. So that when the seed of the word that God has released through me reached you that it would not fall upon stony ground. It is my prayer that you go from becoming a hearer of the word, to a doer of the word. (James 1:22)

There was a man in the Bible named Mephiboseth (II Samuel 4:4; 9:1-13). When Mephiboseth was just a little boy his father and grandfather were both killed in battle. The only one remaining to assist him was a nurse. As the nurse took off running attempting to escape with the little boy on her hip so that the enemies that killed his father and grandfather would not seek out to kill him, she dropped him, deforming both of his legs. There were no orthopedic surgeons to correct the breaks in the little boy's legs so he grew with a limp, both legs being deformed. As Mephibosheth remained there in Lodebar (II Samuel 9:4, 5) all broken, the Bible declares that he had no idea that God had already made provisions for him. He had been there so long that he didn't even know that anyone knew he was there. (II Samuel 9) Not only did God raise him up, but he was able to sit at the king's table and enjoy the wealth of the king without doing anything to make himself be noticed.

Mephiboseth's mind was shaped by what he went through. Even after the king had sent for him to come before him, he still asked the king who am I that you would even take notice of a dirty dog like me. (II Samuel 9:8) Years had passed and he was a grown man, but he still saw himself as a broken little boy. Many people feel like their lives stopped at the time they were the most broken, and so did I. Nobody else has to die for you to gain your inheritance and be blessed. When I say nobody else, I say that because God sent His only son to die that He may be the *propitiator for your sins. A *propitiator is one who takes on the penalty for an act that they did not commit all so that the guilty party can walk free. Your actions have declared you guilty, but when He was crucified on Calvary all charges were dropped. God thought of you, long before you were formed in your mother's womb, He had plans for your life. It may not look like it, but God's got YOU on His mind. (Jeremiah 29:11)

You're blessed when you believe yourself to be so. I don't care what your current situation looks like; I know what the end is going to be. Though your situation may look totally opposite of being blessed - you are. You have to walk out on nothing, and believe that something is there. Your outcome is far greater than your circumstance. We know that when two or three gather together in His name, that He is in the midst, (Matthew 18:20) so in my spirit, I touch and agree with you. If no one else is praying for you, baby, I am.

Even before this reaches you, I feel the anointing of God being released through me. In this release there WILL be a change. I bind the very works of the enemy, that he may no longer cause confusion in your mind, no longer will there be inconsistency in your home, no longer will there be division in your marriage, you will no longer face lack of respect on your job, nor struggle in your finances, or whatever your issue may be. You make yourself be found faithful in your suffering. Press past what others have called you, press past your childhood fears. RELEASE those cries from within!! Pour out yourself to God, so that He can fill those broken places, and bind up the wounds of your spirit. (Psalm 147:2). You are well on your way to releasing those cries from within!

Ten

Holy Visitation

> *Are not all angels ministering spirits sent to serve those who will inherit salvation?*
> **(Hebrews 1:14, NIV)**

I tried my best to move past this hurt, but every day brought another reminder and left me feeling more hopeless than the day before. I grew tired of numerous visits to the guidance counselor's office and passing notes to my English teacher and friends asking for help. Writing became more than an assignment it literally became my saving grace. There was freedom when I put pencil to paper. My thoughts just rolled out even when I did not want them to, and there was no one judging what I wrote.

I had met a new friend at my church that always went out of the way to encourage me and keep me reminded that it wouldn't always be this way. My life took an unexpected turn when she extended the invitation to come to a revival service with her. She went on and on about how good it felt to be in God's presence and to hear people praising God without condemnation. She may as well have said all of this in Spanish because it was foreign to me. The only sound in the churches that I visited was the rustling of pages as we turned our hymnals, heels softly tapping on the hardwood floor beneath our feet, and harmonious voices as the choir sung.

I was intrigued. Church was always my place of refuge, so I could never get enough. Sure! Let's go. Even though I agreed to go, the issue was not having to convince me, but it was my grandmother I would have to get through to. Just the thought of asking her a question always made me cringe. I would stand at the door of her bedroom and count to 100 silently every time I had to ask her a question and once I reached the magic number one hundred I would blurt out my request as fast as I could. I braced myself for her answer because I knew it would not come without some repercussions.

"Grandma, do you mind if I go to revival tonight?" I asked.

"We don't have revival tonight, what are you talking about?"

"No ma'am, I wanted to go to revival with Jeaneen."

"What's so special about revival at that church?"

"Nothing special. I just want to go to church?"

"Why so you can tell somebody else how bad we mistreat you?"

"No ma'am. I just wanted to go to…"

She went from laying to standing as she yelled and fussed about how I never want to stay home, and I'm always in somebody's face.

"I don't care Nefateri. Go! Just stop aggravating me." She stated.

I wasn't concerned about how I got the yes, I was just glad that I could go. I rushed back to the phone to find out what I needed to do and what time to be ready. After we laughed and scheduled my ride for 7:00 PM that evening I hang up the phone so that I could start getting ready.

Time never seems to go fast enough when you are anxious for something to take place. I couldn't explain just what my heart felt, but I almost wanted to stand at the door with my bible and purse in hand and bolt out of it when it was time, but the clock reflected a two hour wait that wouldn't make my standing in the doorway any less nail-biting. The last thing I wanted to do was upset my grandma and have her change her mind.

When my ride showed up they didn't have to extend their southern courtesy of blowing the horn to find out if I was ready.

"Bye Grandma!" I yelled on my way out the door.

Our ride to church was spent talking mostly about previous revival nights that she had already attended, and this made me more anxious than before. When we pulled up on the parking lot of the church it was no mystery that they were having church as the organ, drums, and singing pulled you from your car to the church door. When we walked inside my stomach turned in knots as I looked around the congregation to see hands lifted, people dancing in the aisles, and faces of others who looked like they actually wanted to be there. I sank down into a pew near the back of the sanctuary just in case I wanted to step out. Not only were there lots of people, but there were a lot of people my age. I mostly watched that night, but I could honestly say that I had never encountered such exuberant praise and worship.

When it was time for the word a female Pastor centered the pulpit and preached a message that made me feel like she had been reading my journal. I could not stop myself at this point. The tears streaked down my cheeks and I wept silently. I could feel a tug on my heart and remember thinking no one ever told me how to respond to this. I watched as others were leaping from their seat in tears, or being pulled to their feet as the message touched their hearts as well. I was shaken from my momentary stare as a woman came up to me and extended her hand towards me as if to ask me to follow her. I shook my head no because I had no clue who she was. Her persistence led me to believe that maybe I should follow her. So reluctantly I responded to join her and we began to run hand in hand around the sanctuary. When I looked behind me I realized that several others had joined us.

I remember wondering how long should I run, and where exactly was I running to? But somewhere between thinking and running I begin to focus on the message and all the things that I had endured and I released my doubt and fear and enjoyed that moment in God's presence as I ran.

Even as I relive this revival service I become overwhelmed with the fact that God loved me enough to speak to me that night. It would take growth and maturity for me to realize exactly what He was saying, but I knew that I had walked into something that I never ever wanted to walk away from. There are moments when God stops us in the midst of all of life's worries and frustrations and He reminds us that He loves us. This life-turning moment spoke volumes of Psalm 150:6 as it boldly declares let everything that hath breath praise the Lord. I can't tell you the last time that I had felt so free.

Even though my friend invited me to revival what she unknowingly did was invite me to walk into the truth of how free I could be in God. My life was forever changed.

I was convinced just as the preceding scripture (Hebrews 1:14) that God had sent angels to minister to me that night. And because I know God does not show favoritism, you holding this book means that He has dispatched His ministering angels to you. He wants you to be reminded that He has not forgotten about you. When we struggle and suffer outside of a relationship with God there is a sense of hopelessness, but in Christ there is hope. This hope doesn't just assure you of better days on this side of earth, but in the eternal rest of Heaven. So, I want to extend the opportunity for you too to grab my hand in the spirit and let us run. This lap is one of victory. And while we are running we are shedding the weight of our past trials and experiences that have for so long held us back. I celebrate with you that the intent of the trial to cause you to quit or give up did not work. Let us run with patience (the will and the ability to endure suffering without complaining) the race that is set before us. (Hebrews 12:1, KJV)

Eleven

Pulling Up The Rug

> *Do not participate in the unfruitful deeds of darkness, but instead even expose them;*
> **(Ephesians 5:11, NKJV)**

That one night revival turned into many more nights of revival. Talk of the revival became a common topic in the halls of our high school and lunch conversations. Many of my classmates and I confessed the sinners prayer (Romans 10:9, 10) and became Christians. I thought this life change would bring joy to the hearts of my close family. Instead I was criticized for thinking I was "better than everyone else" or a new member in a cult. Several members of the church tried to talk with my grandmother to help her in understanding what this conversion meant to me. I fought to protect the peace that I had gained on the altar as I cried out to God. There were always events for the young people to be involved and come to develop a personal relationship with God. After asking my grandmother months later for the opportunity to hang out with some of my saved friends I found myself back at another crossroad.

"Grandma, is it okay if I go with some of my church friends to watch a movie?" I asked.

"It's already late where are you watching a movie at?"

"We were going to go to Jeaneen's grandmothers' house. She said it was okay if I came if you didn't mind."

"I tell you what, just go ahead and stay overnight because I don't want no young girl ringing my doorbell all times of the night."

I wasn't arguing with that. An overnight visit? Maybe she had come around and knew that I had proven myself to her. I started into the bedroom to gather my clothes. I thought I'd better hurry up and pack before she changed her mind. I was just settling my last piece of clothing into my overnight bag when she marched up to me.

"You know what! Take all of your stuff and just leave. I'm sick of all the drama you are bringing on this family. You are always having people come over here to talk to me like I'm doing something to hurt you. If you don't want to be here just say you don't want to be here. As a matter of fact you can just get out."

I had heard this so many times before, and to be honest this is merely the clean version of what was actually said to me. And for some apparent reason, I had grown so numb to the yelling, swearings, and telling off that I made up in my mind that I would not only stand still to listen to what she said, but I will take her up on her advice. So that night I chose not to come back. I took the one overnight bag with one set of clothing and it broke my heart, but I knew that if I returned back to that house that what peace I had found would be sifted away.

I laid my head in my best friends lap and I literally cried myself to sleep. I didn't ask to be there and for sure I was not an unruly teenage girl. All I wanted was to be loved and I was always made to feel like this was way too much to ask. I decided that maybe a talk with the Pastor would offer some much needed guidance. After conversing with my best friends' grandmother she offered me to stay with her for the summer since her granddaughters would already be there. I accepted the invitation, but I still needed some spiritual guidance.

I was sure to arrange for an after service meeting. Sitting in the office chair waiting on Bishop Davis to talk with me was nerve wrecking. As I was sitting there I began to second-guess myself. Maybe this wasn't really the best decision. Yet as I was thinking she walked into the office.

"Hey baby, how you are?" she said as she reached to give me a hug.

"I'm okay." I said nervously.

"So, the ushers told me that you needed to talk to me. Have a seat."

Looking down at the floor I begin fidgeting with my fingers as I mumbled, "I'm having problems at home."

"What kind of problems are you having?" she asked inquisitively.

I didn't mean to cry, but just thinking about what I had endured brought me to tears. She waited patiently as I struggled to come up with the words.

"You know I knew your mother." she said.

"You did?" I asked, but I was more surprised that she knew who I was.

She nodded her head yes. I almost felt relieved to talk at this point. She knew my mom? So, I should be able to talk to her. I spent the next moments crying and getting out a word here and there regarding my situation. After our conversation Bishop Davis prayed a prayer over my life that yielded so much compassion. This made me become more and more broken. I arrived at her church several months prior as a seventeen year old teenager, but if I could be honest I was a 5'7" three year old that had never resolved the death of her mom and all of the other hurdles had only complicated my being free.

Bishop Davis did more than talk to me that night. Weeks later she provided me with a place to stay, and helped put me through Cosmetology school. My showing up at revival was no mere coincidence it was a Divine encounter set up by God. And I was so glad that I accepted the request. The love that my church family showed me confirmed that God was doing more than sitting in heaven shouting back at us as though He was a glorified cheerleader cheering on His favorite team. Instead I came to realize that Gods will had already been purposed for me, but it was my responsibility to align myself to what God was saying and not what I wanted to hear Him say.

So how do you align yourself to Gods will? It has to start with finding a bible teaching, God fearing church home where you can attend service and begin to grow. This is the first step. We often excuse not attending a church because we have been offended at our houses of worship or we have witnessed the mishandling of church affairs or other members, but let us be reminded that every patient admitted into a hospital is sick and this does not change the fact that the hospital was established to administer medication to promote physical healing. So regardless of those who have passed away at this same hospital, or how many people received a diagnosis of illness, we too, show up at this facility when we cannot treat our symptoms at home to receive treatment to be made well. Likewise, houses of worship are established to promote healing regardless of how many sin sick are in the pews. I encourage you to focus less on the members and more on Christ.

When I chose not to go back home I remember saying to myself, what in the world am I going to do? But have you ever felt so beat down that you felt like you couldn't get any lower than where you already were? This is where I was. If I stayed I felt as though I would die and if I failed trying, at least I had tried. I have fallen many times as a Christian, but I quickly learned that the beauty wasn't in my falling but in the fact that God had given me the grace to get up from my fall.

Staying where I was could no longer be an option because I felt myself getting lost in the river of toxic words. Toxic words are crippling. Many times we wonder why we don't strive for greatness, or what makes us settle in life. Often if you think back there were comments made about you, words spoken over you, or just an all-out verbal attack made that forced us into believing it was true. We determine this by examining if we have now aligned ourselves to the words that were designed to break us down. I limped around for years in defeat because of toxic words. I cried many nights just imagining just what others saw that caused them to say such negative things about me. When I wearied myself of feeling sorry for myself I begin to submerge myself in God's word. I didn't want to look like the ugliness of what others had spoken; I chose to mirror the excellence of God's word instead. So I allowed the refreshing of His Holy Spirit to breathe new life into me and the only time I look back now is in reflection for how far God has brought me from.

Twelve

Soul Ties

And if one member suffers, all the members suffer with it; or if one member is honoured, all the members rejoice with it.
(I Corinthians 12:26(a), NKJV)

I would spend the next few years grounding my feet in the soil of good Christian teaching and disciplines. I still had a long way to go in order to get through all of my hurts and disappointments, but I was well on my way to total healing. I found myself in a couple of meaningful relationships along the way, but none that I desired to remain in. I allowed my walls of mistrust to be brought low as I welcomed others into my life and into my heart.

When leaving service one Friday night I received a small slip of paper from one of my church brothers with his number and he asked that I give him a call. I took a few days to contact him because I was unsure of what he "really" wanted, but when I did make contact he didn't waste any time letting me know his intent. I had spent many services laughing at his crazy jokes and enjoying his conversation, but I never viewed him as more than a friend. Yet he was asking for the opportunity to get to know me intimately.

After our phone conversation he continued with small gifts and poetry that he would write that left me smiling and open for more. Our dating time was short and I was overwhelmed not only by his friendship but by the host of his other family members that embraced me as their own as well. We went on to marry less than a year later, and the birth of one child was shortly followed by baby boy number two. Even though I had concerns for several long lapses of time when he was coming home in the afternoons, unexplained friends, and stories that just did not add up – I was just glad he came home at night.

It didn't take me long to realize that I still had insurmountable trust issues and I relied heavily on his reassurance of never leaving. I jumped into this relationship with both feet as I looked for him to become so much more than my husband. I had allowed the precedence of this relationship to even take the place of my relationship with God. I eventually stopped going to church, and my hours of church services and bible classes were replaced with house parties, smoking weed, and tall bottles of alcohol.

Stability became a foreign word to us as our marital history brought with it mounting bills, home evictions, court fines and fees, and the steady cleanup of bouncing checks. I wearied holding on to the relationship, but I refused to let go because no other marriage in my immediate family ever made it and I refused to be one in the number. When times became extremely hard on a few occasions one or the other of us would leave to take up temporary residence elsewhere until things would calm down.

I would be awakened in the middle of the night from dreams that left me confused on their meaning, but I was too afraid to pray for God to explain just what He was showing me. One dream halted me enough to get my attention. The dream began with me laying in my spouse's lap crying as I asked him over and over, "how could you do this to me?" I remember the heart-wrenching pain of brokenness that I felt and I stood up in the dream and walked into our bedroom. When I pulled back the covers there were several pools of blood that were smeared all over our sheets and there were handprints everywhere. I awoke from my sleep with my heart pounding, and though I was not sure what it meant, I was aware that neither the handprints nor the blood belonged to me.

I struggled to bring up the dream and I knew that even if I addressed it with him the truth would probably not be shared. However, I had long had this gut feeling that there were more than he and I involved at this point in our relationship. I ignored my gut feeling and chose to stay regardless of what I perceived. On several occasions we relocated hoping that a new location and newfound friends would assist us in moving forward together. Yet, we both learned that the location of a leopard only changes its territory, but the leopards' spots will always remain the same. The one person you will never outrun is self. So everywhere we went we took our issues with us, and slowly but surely we would find ourselves back at square one.

When we neared our sixth year of marriage I felt confident that life was settling. Three years prior I wearied myself of the on-again off-again commitment to God, and I rededicated my life to the Lord. We were able to find a ministry to become a part of, and here I was picking back up where I had previously left off in pursuing my relationship with God. Just three months prior I was ordained for ministry, and what better time than now to ensure that our lives were aligned with the will of God. Our plans of an anniversary trip would be just the thing we needed to renew our relationship with each other. But on the day that we would leave we were both forced to make a decision to move forward or call the relationship what it really was for the both of us – a cover up. I could tell he was broken and I needed to be there for him for the issues he was facing.

So I reached forth my hand to begin to pray in and intercede for him to overcome the issues he felt forced to face, but he retaliated as he grabbed my hand and ensured me that my compassion for him was not warranted or deserved.

It was my endeavor to remain in this union despite the obstacles that threatened to suck the life out of us. Yet in the months to come, it became more and more evident that my spouse's lifestyle and his relentless state of denial caused the kids and I to take a backseat to what really mattered to him. The last thread of this union had finally ripped. I watched as he became farther and farther removed from his family, and more involved with outside distractions.

To be honest, I was holding onto a relationship that had long ejected me from the seat of unity way before I was willing to acknowledge it. The ongoing lies and deceit masked the reality of what I thought I had. So I walked away with an assured peace in my heart that all attempts were made at staying the course. I learned many valuable lessons in it all. One of which was that I was not totally healed from many of the incidents of abuse that I encountered prior to the marriage. And because neither of us had a clue as to what marriage entailed our union only complicated our own personal struggles even more. Instead of seeking Gods word for all of my issues, I became great at only asking Him to help me with the situations I could not control. I do take responsibility for what I did, but it did not excuse what had been done to me.

Relationships take two willing parties and too often we remain in unhealthy relationships as we drag along our children for the ride. We never stay because we want to cause damage, but our selfish nature paints a picture that is really not there. I often attempt to visualize the Garden of Eden. (Genesis 1-3) It was aligned with beautiful trees containing succulent fruit by the numbers that was way more than enough for the two people who inhabited it to consume. However, the selfish nature of man drew Eve to become overwhelmed with the thought of having the one thing God ordered her not to have. The Bible teaches us that when we are tempted we are drawn away at our own lust. (James 1:14) Before Satan tempted Eve she had already longed to eat of the forbidden tree. I am sure the fruit did not taste any better than any of the other fruit. And even if it did, it was masked by the guilt of knowing she was doing something she was already told not to do.

The same loving God who gave instructions still abides faithful in His character today. He watched Eve indulge in disobedience, and He watched Adam follow suit. He never attempted to stop them because God wants us to choose to obey Him, and not be forced. Like Eve I followed my own course in entering into this marriage. I had my own reasons and as a result I had to swallow down the effects of my decision with a good heaping mound of guilt. I could choose to be resentful towards my ex-husband and not forgive, but training our children up in the way they should go (Proverbs 22:6) constitutes more than taking them to church. If they were going to learn forgiveness they would learn it by watching me. If they were going to learn to accept responsibility for their actions, they would learn it by watching me. They needed to know that love keeps no records of wrong so that you deal with one another from a place of hate. (I Corinthians 13:4-7) So, I chose to walk in peace and forgiveness so that I could leave a legacy for my children that far exceeds a healthy bank account. I taught them a lesson on true love and forgiveness. As I moved forward in my new journey of singleness I learned to fall in love with me and who God had made me to be, and it became my goal to not allow anyone to ever mar the reflection of Christ that I endeavor to mirror.

Etched into my spirit
Carved into my soul
Was a holy matrimony
That I thought would make me whole
But I needed from him
The very thing that he needed from me
Yet it wasn't enough to patch the holes
Of our insecurities
Our love tango was like binge drinking
Our consistent need was to just get high
We thought the euphoria of having another human being
Would silence the struggles that we hid inside
But we couldn't seem to drown out the repetition
Of our hum drum heart breaking melodies
So we patched them over with whatever or whoever we could
Pushing us further and further away from our dreams
He couldn't give me what I really needed
He couldn't heal this heart that always ached
I couldn't answer his never ending questions
I couldn't right the wrongs of his countless mistakes
There was a love affair we couldn't compete with
One that was destined to tear us apart
We were never really naked and ashamed as God intended
In the end, we were married to what
The baggage our past had produced
Left us calloused, hearts bruised, and hopes tarred
But in the end though our paths each went separate ways
Knowing I still had my Redeemer was my reward.

Thirteen

Breaking Free

> *In my anguish I cried to the LORD, and He answered by setting me free.*
> **(Psalm 118:5, NKJV)**

There was one character attribute that I came to realize that I was lacking in and that was contentment. I was always living for the next moment and it left me discontented where I was. The closing of one chapter would not be complete before I was ripping open the pages of the next. I decided one evening that the cracking sound of my apartment walls reminded me more and more of what my life sounded like because everything around me was crashing down. Whenever the silence around you seems to scream loudly it's time to take a break. So I loaded my boys into the car and decided we should go for a ride.

"Mommy where are we going?" my eldest son Allen asked. "Just sit tight man, we are going for a ride, ok?" I said.

"Are we going a long way?" Clifton, my youngest, joined in with his questions.

"Guys, I just needed to get out of the house for a while so just ride." I concluded.

Either they were wearied of me not really answering their questions or they heard what I wasn't saying and not what I did say. Whichever resolve they came to, it kept them both quiet for some time. While on my own as a single parent I worked a fairly decent job, but my lack of financial management sent me into a whirlwind of evictions and final notices from other bill collectors. I had more debt than I had income and my spending habits were not the best.

So much for the thought of leaning on others for support because it sometimes came with a guilt trip and my pride didn't feel like being squeezed on that day. We rolled down the car windows and the boys squealed as loudly as they could from the backseat as they hid under jackets trying to make a tent in the car. This was one of their pastimes when riding – trying to outsmart the breeze that was being let into the windows.

If we were in the car for more than five minutes I could rest assured that one of them would beg me,

"Mommy, roll the windows all the way down."

I was just glad they were happy. But at that moment I couldn't say the same for me. The mounds of hurt abuse, and disappointment had outgrown the rug that I was trying to sweep it under. I couldn't hide it anymore. After driving for almost half of an hour I neared a bridge and I pulled over momentarily because the tears that filled my eyes were blinding my vision to see. I had failed, yet again, but this time with two sets of eyes looking up to me. I looked over my shoulder as I noticed there was no longer any laughter from my backseat only to realize that both boys had fallen asleep.

As I covered them up under their jackets just slightly, my mind flashed to the moment when my brother and I were this small and we too were a year apart just like my boys. I cried even more as I begin to consider how my failed marriage had now robbed them of a two-parent home as well. Why wouldn't anything ever work for me? I loved God and I served Him without restraint. I wasn't perfect, but I was committed. I turned around and begin to talk to the Lord:

"Lord how can you allow me to go on like this? I am so tired of being hurt and let down. I can't go anymore. I don't want to go anymore. My heart is so broken. I am so ashamed of the mess I have made. I am tired of struggling. I didn't ask for this. I didn't ask for this." I repeated.

As I poured my heart out to God I just begin to think that this world would be so much better without me in it. Instead of being the burden I felt I was to so many others, I could just check out on life and there would be no more pain. I had concluded that night that suicide was the best option. But how would I succeed at this? As I looked around me I noticed that I had pulled over right at the foot of a bridge. There was no way I could leave my children behind and have the same thing happen to them that happened to me. I didn't want another family member to take them into custody and not treat them as they should. I knew the devastation of waking every morning in a home where you are made to feel like a burden, and I didn't want that for my children.

My decision was made; I could drive over the side of this bridge with my kids in the car and do away with us all. Yes! Yes! I was almost excited at the thought of having figured this all out. I immediately started thinking of my family and friends and what they would think or what they would have to say, and sadly enough I don't think that any of them would even care. I grabbed my cell phone and I thought to myself, let me at least call and hear my mom, Bishop Davis', voice just one last time.

When she answered I could tell she was resting and in that moment I thought, should I have even bothered her right now; she sounded tired. My thought was interrupted as I heard her say again, "Hello??"

"Oh, hey Ma. How are you doing?" I asked trying to sound as normal as possible.

"I'm doing good baby. How are you?"

"I'm doing good."

There was a brief pause after my last response.

"Are you okay Nep?" she said. Nep was the affectionate name she called me.

"Uhmm. Yes ma'am."

"No, something isn't right. Where are you right now?"
"I'm in my car."

"Okay where are you going, it's kind of late for you to be out."

"I was just riding." I responded.

I really wanted to hang up. Maybe calling her was not the best thing to do.

"Nep. I can tell something is going on with you and I am not sure what it is, but let's just pray okay."

I didn't respond. And before I could, she began praying aloud. The tears were rolling down my cheeks so fast that attempting to wipe them did no good. I was tossed in that moment. Do I just disregard her words or do I gather the

strength to accelerate and drive over this bridge wh..
on the phone? I know Bishop Davis couldn't see me an.
did my best to muffle the warfare that I had going on in that
moment so why not ignore the prayer and just go through
with it? My spirit cried aloud but I cried quietly. The more
she prayed I could feel life and hope coming back into me.
I resisted the urge to hang up the phone and I sat and listened as she prayed.

It would be years later before I even told her what happened
that night. Yet, just like our first meeting, this moment was
a Divine intervention. I didn't really want to die, but in that
moment I didn't feel the need to live. After I gathered myself and my thoughts I drove back to my apartment. When
I had settled both boys into bed I laid across my bed in the
quiet and I asked God to forgive me for wanting to give up.
I asked God that night to help me not go any further in life
without allowing Him to heal me completely from the issues that plagued me from my past.

I don't know what bothered me more; seeing myself in the
state I was in or knowing that I deserved so much better.
Ecclesiastes 3:11 states that God makes all things beautiful in his time. So, I decided to join in with God and allow
myself to be made beautiful. I made a vow that night that I
would no longer live in one moment longing for the next,
but I wanted God to get the glory out of my life. I prayed
that this season of my life would be maximized so that others would come to see and know the work of Christ in me.

Here are some amazing statistics for you:

Marital status is associated with suicide risk. Living alone
and being single both increase the risk of suicide. Marriage

is associated with lower overall suicide rates; and divorced, separated and widowed people are more likely to commit suicide. Gender seems to affect this relationship; divorced and widowed men are more likely than divorced and widowed women to commit suicide.

http://www.hsccs.org

I am not alluding to the fact that this is ALL due to ones' marital status. Statistics gives us these numbers and please know that every suicidal success isn't done only by those who are not Christian believers. Grace overrides the statistics, but unfortunately not everyone walks in that grace. Over the past few years the numbers of postings that have entered my own personal newsfeed on social media of Christians committing suicide is alarming. I often stop to whisper a prayer for the families involved knowing that it is only by God's grace that there was not a newsfeed that read of me and my kids. Having to go through divorce from a spouse parallels death. There is a part of you that feels missing, and no matter what happened on your part or theirs, you are left to grieve the happily ever after.

Life in and of itself can be overwhelming, but let me reassure you that had it not been for me surrounding myself with others who could pray me through some difficult seasons or for the many seasons I had to pray for myself, you might have read my story, but it would not have been written by me. It seems much easier to blame others for the state in which we find ourselves, but pointing fingers never works. Instead of using your hands to point your finger in accusation I would encourage you to try lifting your hands towards heaven as a sign of surrender.

I replaced phone conversations with prayer time. I replaced

complaining for giving God praise. Instead of allowing the quicksand of hopelessness to hold me still I replaced it with a dancing in my feet for the Lord. I decided to become the mother to my boys that I too needed at their age. Internally I swept up the dirt that was under my emotional rug and I handed it to God. He honored His word as He gave me beauty for the ashes of my past, the oil of joy for mourning, and a garment of praise for the spirit of heaviness. (Isaiah 61:3) I learned in that season that walking in freedom is a choice, and by God I wanted to be free. Do you? If so, let us dance together in the spirit knowing that what hurt you no longer hinders you.

Freedom brings with it a great responsibility because Gods testament becomes evident for others to see as they look at your life. There is responsibility that comes along with anything that yields power including our influence. Our first and foremost desire should be to please God. I had gained a freedom, but my freedom walk was travelled with a few hitchhikers that I hoped to ignore. If I was to truly walk upright I knew there were some issues that had to be dismantled no matter the cost. The hitchhikers that plagued me the most was my overwhelming feelings of loneliness and low self-esteem. I could quote you scriptures, lead you into prayer, and teach you a bible lesson, but when I was alone these hitchhikers did their best to convince me that they would win. And to be honest, there were times and seasons when they were winning.

I didn't want to close the door on my issues or set up boundaries to not find myself in situations that would allow me to compromise Gods will for my life, so I had merely become a functioning Christian. Many functioning Christians are not pretending in their relationships with God. They really have a desire to live upright and to lead others. Yet the internal warfare plays tug-of-war with their will to do what's right. I intended to walk in freedom, but I just didn't want to face the voids that were there. I matured into knowing that your calling doesn't exempt you from struggle, but instead you become a prime target for the enemy so that he might disqualify Gods' testimony in and over your life.

After my divorce I had allowed my insecurities to place me in the arms of men that could never really hold me in the first place, but at the time my desire to be held outweighed my desire to do the right thing. I justified my actions by saying to myself, "it's not like I'm going to die." And when I found myself entangled in these meaningless relationships I asked God how in the world did I get here?? He quickly reminded me of this very same conversation I had with myself months prior that giving myself over to the lust of my flesh would not kill me. Yet when He reminded me, I was also reminded of the serpents' conversation with Eve in Genesis 3:4 when he encouraged her to eat the fruit from the forbidden tree for she will not certainly die. We believe the lies of the enemy and many people get stuck here because we begin to deem ourselves worthless because of bad choices that we have made, but I am so glad that God died with me in mind. Romans 5:8 says that God demonstrated His loved towards us: while we were yet sinners Christ died for us. This was just the motivation I needed to break free. So instead of pretending my issues were not there I had to stand before the mirror and face some giants that I had nursed way too long. (James 1:24) Pretending I had no struggle or tucking it away in the back of my mental closet as if it was not there, did not constitute dealing with my issues.

It was at the moment that I chose to confess before God, and submit myself to others who would hold me accountable as I recovered that I would truly be free. I had only hoped that because God called me that He had already forgiven me for my actions, but the gifts and callings of God (whatever He has called you to do) is without repentance, (Romans 11:29), however if we choose not to deal with our closet skeletons we leave them lying around for others to trip over the bones of our past that we carelessly leave behind.

Oftentimes our church pulpits and pews are filled with men and women who hope to cover their issues and not lay bare before God to be made free. Should you haphazardly run around exposing your issues to anyone who would give sight or sound to what you have gone through; indeed not. But neither should we play Russian roulette with our own lives and those in which we are connected. Russian roulette is a game where a bullet is placed in the chamber of the gun and we take turns pointing the gun at ourselves or others in hopes that the bullet isn't unloaded in us. I encourage you to fight hard to break free knowing that if we confess our faults one to another that He is faithful and just to forgive us and cleanse us from unrighteousness. (I John 1:9) You are valuable to the kingdom. Your discomfort to stay put, and not allow God to heal you is the Holy Spirits' reminder to you that it is time to be free. Let us take this walk of freedom together.

Fourteen

Escaped To Tell

> *But I have prayed for you, that your faith fail not: and when you are converted, strengthen your brothers.*
> **(Luke 22:32, AKJV)**

I went on in Gods purpose for my life. I choked down the overwhelming desire to be disappointed in myself. Each day became a little less difficult than the day before. I would spend the next three and a half years of my life embracing the call to Pastor. Each lesson I taught and every sermon that I delivered was taught with great mercy and conviction to see others better than what they were when I met them. If anything I felt even more empowered because of the things that I had endured to help the hurting and the lost. The storefront church in which we held services may not have offered the luxury of a grand church home, but the love and fellowship found within was without mention. I was also glad to know that my divorce from my ex-husband did not sever the ties with my newfound family that I married into. They often reminded me that their love and support would not change despite his decision. I am a firm believer in listening to what people say, while watching what they do. Their words were not empty because they often went above and beyond what they said. My in-laws supported me both emotionally and financially as they still do to this day. When either myself or my boys were sick I could expect a knock at the door that was followed by a suitcase as my Mom and Dad made sure that their presence would always be there.

About two years into pastoring I remember praying to God on my way home from one of our church services. I leaned over on my driver's door on my arm that was perched atop and I said aloud, "God, I don't want to do this by myself anymore. I want a companion that I can share in ministry with. I want someone who is excited to have me come home after a long day. I want my boys to have a father in their lives that will speak life into them and prepare them to be men." For the first time I wasn't praying this prayer from a place of desperation – I really longed to have a companion. When I was done praying, I continued home. It would be almost a year later that God answered my quiet prayer while driving home from service that day.

I had prematurely opened myself up to two potentials that left me at a mindset of not wanting to even open that door again. As soon as I learned of their interest I would be so consumed at the idea of the possibility of marriage that it would blind my judgment to the substance of whether this was really worth my time. I wearied of getting to know someone else. But my sisters' three months of persistence gave me hope to at least enjoy a nice date.

So I met with this prospective mate for movies and dinner and the rest is absolute history. For the first time EVER I had met a man that actually cared about me, and not what I could offer him. He lived almost two hours away, but it was nothing for him to drive up after his work hours to make repairs to our church, service my car, or make sure that I was okay. Not only did he care about me, but he too was a Pastor and his compassion for Gods' people was just as pure as my own. We knew that this Divine connection would lead to so much more than dating.

When I told him of my past he didn't judge me, instead he encouraged me.

"I fell in love with you, and we know that our lives are all made up of negatives and positives. If you were not genuine in who you were, God would not have led me to you. Is your past over?" he asked.

With tears rolling down my face, I could only work up a "yes."

"Well let's move forward. You didn't have a covering before, but you have one now."

I was finally at a place where I knew what I wanted, but more importantly what God wanted for me. After extending my hand in acceptance to his proposal for marriage we agreed to continue in ministry together. I needed that someone who could be prophet (pointing our family in the right direction towards God), priest (rules over his home with reverence for God and authority against the enemy and his assignments), and king (a man who knew who he was in God while walking in Gods leadership and serving others as he went). I brought to our union two handsome priests, and he brought three beautiful princesses of his own. We have embarked on territory together in ministry that we would have otherwise never known before meeting each other. Wisdom has led us to stay submitted first of all to Christ, and subsequently surrounding ourselves with others who seek to bring glory to God through their service to the kingdom.

In my journey to wholeness the Holy Spirit nudged me to read the book of Job. Anyone who knows Job struggles knows my apprehension of flipping the pages of my Bible to this book. I struggled to be obedient because I felt like God was preparing me to go through yet another storm. However, I was unable to escape this inner nudge to read. So after settling my children in one night I decided to grab my Bible and see just what it was that God was trying to show me. I remember reading chapter one and as I went on to read chapter two the Holy Spirit spoke to me and said, "go back and read it again."

I went from lying down and reading to sitting up as I read through chapter one again. I paused for a moment and then lifted my Bible to go on to chapter two when I distinctly heard the Holy Spirit speak to me once more saying, "go back and read it again." At that point, I had to respond. I sat my Bible down on the bed and looked towards heaven and said, "God I don't get it."

I grabbed my Bible and begin to read it aloud, and the words made me stand to my feet as what I was reading begin to make sense to me. I changed my perception the last time I started reading. I initially read out of fear for what God wanted to say to me the first couple times. The last time I began to read I was searching for an understanding of the scripture itself.

The same five words kept appearing over and over in several verses in Job 1:15-17, 19. God begin to reveal to me that night that there were issues in my life that were destined to make me lose my focus, my mind, and my testimony. Yet in all these things I was more than a conqueror. (Romans 8:37) Every time Job lost something be it cattle, possessions, or loved ones, there was one servant that had escaped to bring him the report. I realized that night that I did not die in the midst of my struggles and trials because I too had escaped to tell. I would lose some things and some people along the way, but I would escape to tell about it. And I eventually finished reading of Job's accounts. I was encouraged to know that Job 42:10 disclosed that the Lord gave him twice as much as before. Not only had I escaped, but all that I had lost would be returned to me twofold. I believe we call that double for our trouble. (Isaiah 61:7) I was not necessarily concerned with double possessions, but no one knew my inner turmoil and I longed to just be free in my spirit and walk with true inherent joy.

    We try to hold onto our perceived destiny, but I would love to encourage you to trust God to do only what He can do. I would often question some of the paths in which God had led me, and even the ones in which I walked on my own without seeking Gods will. But I can say with great confidence on today that this message of love, hope, forgiveness, and restoration is being told by one who has walked the dusty roads of defeat, those roads where the only companion were the footsteps of others who had travelled by, or the corpses of those who had never made it. I have pulled the knives of betrayal from my back, and sat as the Holy Spirit cleansed my wounds as I cried like a baby from the pain of no anesthesia to numb me. I've watched as Satan took invested relationships and made them enemies, but I take joy in it all. I am now walking into my promised land with no bitterness and no regrets.

Every man that failed me was another reason for the enemy to keep me bound and cause me to only identify my Heavenly Father through lives' misperceptions, but TODAY I am whole and I am healed and you may not know Job, but I, Nefateri Pecou Smalls, has escaped to tell you that your God is not only willing, but able to heal you. And beyond your healing, God is forgiving. He will allow you the grace to forgive others who have wronged you, while at the same time extending you the grace to do what many others find impossible and that is to forgive yourself. Will you believe?

You must know that in order to escape, you are breaking free from confinement or control; surpassing restraint; to gain or regain liberty. You deserve to get past where you are and move on to where God would have you to be, and today I hand you your key to freedom because you too have escaped to tell.

Scriptures Noted in the Text

Genesis 41:51
Joseph called the name of the firstborn Manasseh: "For God has made me forget all my toil and all my father's house."

Genesis 50:20
But as for you, you meant evil against me; but God meant it for good, in order to bring it about as it is this day, to save many people alive.

Deuteronomy 8:18
But thou shall remember the LORD thy God: for it is he that giveth thee power to get wealth, that he may establish his covenant which he sware unto thy fathers, as it is this day.

I Samuel 4:4
So the people sent to Shiloh, that they might bring from there the ark of the covenant of the LORD of hosts, who dwells between the cherubim. And the two sons of Eli, Hophni and Phinehas, were there with the ark of the covenant of God.

I Samuel 9:1-13
There was a man of Benjamin whose name was Kish the son of Abiel, the son of Zeror, the son of Bechorath, the son of Aphiah, a Benjamite, a mighty man of power. And he had a choice and handsome son whose name was Saul. There was not a more handsome person than he among the children of Israel. From his shoulders upward he was taller than any of the people. Now the donkeys of Kish, Saul's father, were lost. And Kish said to his son Saul, "Please take

one of the servants with you, and arise, go and look for the donkeys." So he passed through the mountains of Ephraim and through the land of Shalisha, but they did not find them. Then they passed through the land of Shaalim, and they were not there. Then he passed through the land of the Benjamites, but they did not find them. When they had come to the land of Zuph, Saul said to his servant who was with him, "Come, let us return, lest my father cease caring about the donkeys and become worried about us." And he said to him, "Look now, there is in this city a man of God, and he is an honorable man; all that he says surely comes to pass. So let us go there; perhaps he can show us the way that we should go." Then Saul said to his servant, "But look, if we go, what shall we bring the man? For the bread in our vessels is all gone, and there is no present to bring to the man of God. What do we have?" And the servant answered Saul again and said, "Look, I have here at hand one-fourth of a shekel of silver. I will give that to the man of God, to tell us our way." (Formerly in Israel, when a man went to inquire of God, he spoke thus: "Come, let us go to the seer"; for he who is now called a prophet was formerly called a seer.) Then Saul said to his servant, "Well said; come, let us go." So they went to the city where the man of God was. As they went up the hill to the city, they met some young women going out to draw water, and said to them, "Is the seer here?" And they answered them and said, "Yes, there he is, just ahead of you. Hurry now; for today he came to this city, because there is a sacrifice of the people today on the high place. As soon as you come into the city, you will surely find him before he goes up to the high place to eat. For the people will not eat until he comes, because he must bless the sacrifice; afterward those who are invited will eat. Now therefore, go up, for about this time you will find him."

Isaiah 61:3
and provide for those who grieve in Zion—
to bestow on them a crown of beauty instead of ashes, the oil of joy instead of mourning, and a garment of praise instead of a spirit of despair. They will be called oaks of righteousness, a planting of the LORD for the display of his splendor.

Isaiah 61:7
Instead of your shame you will receive a double portion, and instead of disgrace you will rejoice in your inheritance.
And so you will inherit a double portion in your land, and everlasting joy will be yours.

Jeremiah 2:1
Moreover the word of the LORD came to me, saying.

Jeremiah 2:12
For my people have committed two evils; they have forsaken me the fountain of living waters, and hewed them out cisterns, broken cisterns, that can hold no water.

Jeremiah 29:11
For I know the thoughts that I think toward you, says the LORD, thoughts of peace and not of evil, to give you a future and a hope.

Psalm 27:10, 11
When my father and my mother forsake me, then the LORD will take me up.
And Joseph called the name of the firstborn Manasseh: For God, said he, hath made me forget all my toil, and all my father's house.

Psalm 42:5
Why art thou cast down, O my soul? and why art thou disquieted in me? hope thou in God: for I shall yet praise him for the help of his countenance.

Psalm 107:20
He sent His word and healed them, and delivered them from their destructions.

Psalm 118:5
In my anguish I cried to the LORD, and He answered by setting me free.

Psalm 147:2
The LORD doth build up Jerusalem: he gathereth together the outcasts of Israel.

Psalm 150:6a
Let everything that has breath praise the LORD.

Proverbs 18:21
Death and life are in the power of the tongue, And those who love it will eat its fruit.

Proverbs 22:6
Start children off on the way they should go, and even when they are old they will not turn from it.

Proverbs 23:7
For as he thinks in his heart, so is he. "Eat and drink!" he says to you, But his heart is not with you.

Ecclesiastes 3:11
He has made everything beautiful in its time. He has also set eternity in the human heart; yet no one can fathom what God has done from beginning to end.

Job 1:15-17, 19
When the Sabeans raided them and took them away—indeed they have killed the servants with the edge of the sword; and I alone have escaped to tell you!"
While he was still speaking, another also came and said, "The fire of God fell from heaven and burned up the sheep and the servants, and consumed them; and I alone have escaped to tell you!"
While he was still speaking, another also came and said, "The Chaldeans formed three bands, raided the camels and took them away, yes, and killed the servants with the edge of the sword; and I alone have escaped to tell you!" and suddenly a great wind came from across the wilderness and struck the four corners of the house, and it fell on the young people, and they are dead; and I alone have escaped to tell you!"

Job 42:10
And the LORD restored Job's losse when he prayed for his friends. Indeed the LORD gave Job twice as much as he had before.

Song of Solomon 2:7
I charge you, O ye daughters of Jerusalem, by the roes, and by the hinds of the field, that ye stir not up, nor awake my love, till he pleases.

Matthew 6:33-34
But seek ye first the kingdom of God, and his righteous-

ness; and all these things shall be added unto you Take therefore no thought for the morrow: for the morrow shall take thought for the things of itself. Sufficient unto the day is the evil thereof.

Matthew 18:20
For where two or three are gathered together in My name, I am there in the midst of them."

Luke 22:32
But I have prayed for you, that your faith fail not: and when you are converted, strengthen your brothers.

John 7:38
He that believeth on me, as the scripture hath said, out of his belly shall flow rivers of living water.

John 15:2
Now ye are clean through the word which I have spoken unto you.

Acts 17:6
But when they did not find them, they dragged Jason and some brethren to the rulers of the city, crying out, "These who have turned the world upside down have come here too."

Romans 5:8
But God demonstrates His own love toward us, in that while we were still sinners, Christ died for us.

Romans 8:17
And if children, then heirs—heirs of God and joint heirs with Christ, if indeed we suffer with Him, that we may also be glorified together.

Romans 8:28
And we know that all things work together for good to those who love God, to those who are the called according to His purpose.

Romans 8:36, 37
As it is written, For thy sake we are killed all the day long; we are accounted as sheep for the slaughter.
Nay, in all these things we are more than conquerors through him, that loved us

Romans 10:9, 10
If you declare with your mouth, "Jesus is Lord," and believe in your heart that God raised him from the dead, you will be saved. For it is with your heart that you believe and are justified, and it is with your mouth that you profess your faith and are saved.

Romans 11:29
For the gifts and the calling of God are irrevocable.

I Corinthians 12:26(a)
And if one member suffers, all the members suffer with it; or if one member is honoured, all the members rejoice with it.

I Corinthians 13:4-7
Love is patient, love is kind. It does not envy, it does not boast, it is not proud. It does not dishonor others, it is not self-seeking, it is not easily angered, it keeps no record of wrongs. Love does not delight in evil but rejoices with the truth. It always protects, always trusts, always hopes, always perseveres.

Ephesians 5:11
Do not participate in the unfruitful deeds of darkness, but instead even expose them;

Ephesians 6:19, 20
And for me, that utterance may be given unto me, that I may open my mouth boldly, to make known the mystery of the gospel,
For which I am an ambassador in bonds: that therein I may speak boldly, as I ought to speak.

Philippians 1:1
Being confident of this very thing, that he which hath begun a good work in you will perform it until the day of Jesus Christ:

Philippians 1:6
Being confident of this very thing, that He who has begun a good work in you will complete it until the day of Jesus Christ;

Philippians 3:13, 14
Brethren, I do not count myself to have apprehended; but one thing I do, forgetting those things which are behind and reaching forward to those things which are ahead, I press toward the goal for the prize of the upward call of God in Christ Jesus.

Hebrews 1:14
Are not all angels ministering spirits sent to serve those who will inherit salvation?

Hebrews 10:32-35
But call to remembrance the former days, in which, after

ye were illuminated, ye endured a great fight of afflictions; Partly, whilst ye were made a gazingstock both by reproaches and afflictions; and partly, whilst ye became companions of them that were so used. For ye had compassion of me in my bonds, and took joyfully the spoiling of your goods, knowing in yourselves that ye have in heaven a better and an enduring substance Cast not away therefore your confidence, which hath great recompense of reward.

Hebrews 12:1
Therefore, since we are surrounded by such a great cloud of witnesses, let us throw off everything that hinders and the sin that so easily entangles. And let us run with perseverance the race marked out for us.

James 1:14
When tempted, no one should say, "God is tempting me." For God cannot be tempted by evil, nor does he tempt anyone; but each person is tempted when they are dragged away by their own evil desire and enticed. Then, after desire has conceived, it gives birth to sin; and sin, when it is full-grown, gives birth to death.

James 1:22-24
But be ye doers of the word, and not hearers only, deceiving your own selves. For if anyone is a hearer of the word and not a doer, he is like a man observing his natural face in a mirror; for he observes himself, goes away, and immediately forgets what kind of man he was.

John 1:9
If we confess our sins, He is faithful and just to forgive us our sins and to cleanse us from all unrighteousness.

Order Form

Enclosed is my check or money order made payable to Nefateri Smalls.

To assure prompt and accurate delivery of your order, please take the time to print all of your information neatly.

Name _____

Address _____

City _____ State _____

Zip _____

Area Code & Phone ( )_____

Price of book: $12.95 + Shipping and handling $2.00 = $14.95

Send all mail orders to:
Nefateri Smalls
P.O. Box 231
Ridgeville, SC 29472